Paul Frederick Tidman

Gold and Silver Money

Paul Frederick Tidman

Gold and Silver Money

ISBN/EAN: 9783743313583

Manufactured in Europe, USA, Canada, Australia, Japa

Cover: Foto ©ninafisch / pixelio.de

Manufactured and distributed by brebook publishing software (www.brebook.com)

Paul Frederick Tidman

Gold and Silver Money

THE ARGUMENT.

The Silver Question, treated from a practical point of view, is simple and interesting; it affects every individual. Metallic money has superseded barter, and an increase in its volume is necessary as the world's commerce expands, *p.* 5. The value of money consists in its fixity of value, which is the result of its being a patent article made only by the State, *p.* 6. The exchangeable use of money is second only in importance to its adoption by the State as a standard or measure of values, which to be effectual must be permanent and assured, *p.* 10. The State, by creating the demand for the precious metals in the manufacture of money, controls the market for them, *p.* 13. Money, as currency, will have more or less purchasing power according as it is scarce or abundant; but money as the standard of value is unaffected by the amount of the precious metals in circulation, *p.* 25. Gold and silver are universally allowed to be the best standard of value; some nations using one and some both, *p.* 26. A standard based on both must be less liable to variation than if confined to one, *p.* 29. England made a mistake in 1816 by discarding silver as joint base of her Standard, and Germany was similarly at fault in 1873, *p.* 30. The demand for silver being now so much reduced, and its character discredited, its value is falling and fluctuating, *p.* 31. Great danger to the world's commerce, and especially to the trade of England, is admitted to exist in consequence, and the question is, how can the value of silver be restored and made permanent? *p.* 45 The proposal of the Paris Conference of 1878, shown to be impracticable, *p.* 50, as is also an alternative scheme advocated by Professor Bonomy Price, *p.* 64. The proposal of the Bi-metallists stated, *p.* 55. The question can be disposed of, to the great advantage of this country and the benefit of international trade, if England will join a union of the Continental Powers with the United States, *p.* 67.

GOLD AND SILVER MONEY.

PART I.

A PLAIN STATEMENT.

A CABINET MINISTER said last year, to a friend who inquired of him, if he understood 'The Silver Question,' that he had never ventured to go into it, because a theoretical financier, who had studied it for thirteen years, had confessed at the end of that period that he was hopelessly bewildered.

It may seem, therefore, presumptuous to attempt to popularise anything regarded as so abstruse and complicated. And yet, in these days, since almost every science, whether dealing with such phenomena as the transit of

Venus or the fixtures of a drawing-room, has been elucidated in shilling handbooks, there would seem precedent for venturing on a plain statement of one of the greatest questions which arise out of Monetary Science; a question moreover which is pressing for a settlement, and *which affects every individual member of the commonwealth.*

It will be admitted that it is practicable to take an interest in, and understand many phenomena, without having mastered the abstract principles which underlie them, or being equal to making mathematical calculations regarding them. It is so with that practical aspect of Monetary Science, called ' **The Silver Question**,' which is now being so freely discussed, and which will be found both intelligible and interesting, when the disputes which have arisen out of the various definitions of ' Money,' ' Commodities,' and the like, are consigned to oblivion, and the common-sense view of the case (if I may say so without offence to the political economists) becomes the one on which attention is concentrated.

The men who conduct the commerce of the world, the men whose every operation is based upon money, the dealers in money, get but short shrift at the hands of *the dealers in theories about money.* Professor Bonamy Price, one of the ablest of the latter, has just favoured us with a portrait* of the 'practical man,' the author of all confusion, who 'pours out elaborate theories, with the fullest assurance that *he* knows.' The truth is that theoretical economists, as a rule, can see little on the ground beneath them. It is with them, as with the inhabitants of Laputa, of whom Gulliver tells us that in their heads, one eye turned inwards and the other was directed towards the Zenith. Their 'cause and effect—demand and supply' becomes as monotonous as the ticking of a

* *Contemporary Review*, February.

clock. No doubt, if their united wisdom could foresee every cause, they would be guides whom business men would be wise to follow, but a scientific treatise is not found in practice to be the best manual for a counting-house. Causes more varying than the waves of the sea, more subtle than the changes of wind and temperature, affect markets and make the difference between profit and loss. Often, indeed, the scientific formula, 'demand and supply,' brings no more reassurance to business men than it would do to the schoolboy gazing wistfully into the pastrycook's window, when his pocket money was exhausted. It is cold comfort in the midst of a panic to be told that 'confidence ought not to have been shaken,' and that the bank rate 'ought not to have been put up.'

We all prize Money, all strive to acquire it, because it means wealth, which may be best stored in this form, or may be at once exchanged for food, clothing, and luxuries.

To those who use it as the mass of the world do, it becomes indispensable as **currency**, *i.e.* it runs from one hand to another, and it has thus enabled the world to rise out of a state of barbarism, in which the individual could procure commodities only if he happened to be able to offer in exchange an article which was wanted. Metallic money has superseded the primitive modes of barter, because it is itself something which is of use to every one, and can always be exchanged for commodities. Any sudden or rapid diminution in its supply, therefore, must hamper such exchanges, or, in common language, restrict trade, and what is desirable is, **a steady increase of the volume of money, in proportion to the development of the world's requirements.**

But, in what consists its value to those who use it, and to those who store it?

Clearly, in **its fixity of value**; in its **stability.** If Gold were sometimes saleable for one hundred shillings an ounce, and soon afterwards (consequent on the substitution of some new metal in the place of it as Money) worth half the amount, it would at once lose the supreme importance which attaches to it.

What gives Money this unchanging value, which nothing else possesses?

It is a Patent article made by the State, and by no one but the State, and just as, when such raw material as cotton and silk are woven into cloth, the manufactured article differs in its appearance and uses from those it possessed as a mere natural product, so does the **Metal Gold** become transformed in the course of its manufacture into **Money**. As regards appearance, it has now acquired a certain shape and size, and upon it is **the Patent Mark,** 'to imitate which is forgery.' The sovereign has a different use to that which could have been made of the small nugget or pinch of Gold dust, out of which it has been formed. It passes from hand to hand a dozen times a day, without doubt or difficulty, and has become exchangeable for all commodities.

Why?

For this reason: that the Patent Mark of the State guarantees it to uniformly contain the same weight of fine Gold; and, whenever the patentees find a sovereign which has lost in weight, they destroy the coin, by giving it a clip with the bank scissors, thus effectually preventing it from doing duty any more as **Money**. The coin which has been thus defaced, retains the value of whatever weight of Gold it may contain, but as **Money** it has ceased to exist, and must be re-manufactured before it can perform the functions of currency.

So that it becomes evident, that **the State which creates Money, has likewise the power to destroy it.**

But the **exchangeable** or **commercial** use of

Money, is not its only or its primary and distinguishing feature. Compare the Gold dust or the nugget with the sovereign, and mark the ideas upon the two which rise respectively in the mind. The nugget *looks like* Gold, and it may be Gold, but the Patent article *you know* is Gold, because of the Queen's head upon it. The nugget may be large or small, worth £10 or £100, with Gold enough in it to pay for the 'Edition de Luxe' of Thackeray, or a new copy of the 'Encyclopædia Britannica.' It may be small enough to make you doubt whether you can purchase with it a box of cabanas at 80*s.* per hundred, or whether it would defray the cost of a rocking-horse (30*s.*) for your child; but you turn to the coined metal, the sovereign, and become aware that four such pieces will be required to pay for the cigars, and one and a half for the toy.

You have been unconsciously calculating— the calculation being based **upon a fixed**

measure or standard of value accepted by everybody else as well as yourself.

Note, that you have no choice but to accept it. The patentee says you shall do so, and that everybody else shall do so, so that, if you buy the cigars or, better still, *two* rocking-horses for the twins, and the bill for them is sent in at 30s. each, the patentee compels the seller to give a receipt on your handing him three of these sovereigns. Once again, it is manifest that **Money is the creature of law.**

This faculty of **measuring** at once takes Money out of the category of other commodities, entitling it, for all practical purposes, to be spoken of by a name which, while not excluding the idea of a commodity, brings another and a different idea so prominently forward as to put the other out of sight. The change undergone in the manufacture of Money may be illustrated (up to a certain point) by another metal, quicksilver, which is imported in iron flasks, and varies in value from £6 to £20 per flask. Directed into different channels of commerce, this metal deals with you unsparingly in the shape of a pill, and in another form, enables you to watch the effect of that pill upon the face reflected in your mirror. With differing uses, it remains the same commodity. But follow it further, and, as you step into your greenhouse, stop to notice the temperature. The commodity quicksilver is imprisoned in that tube; but is not the first and overpowering association now in your mind with it, one of a **standard or measure?** and is not the worth and use of a thermometer quite a different and distinct worth and use to you than is that of the quicksilver in a flask? The mercury, being a natural product, becomes a measure of temperature in virtue of its obedience to the *laws of nature*, but *Money*, being an artificial production, **acts as a measure under the supremacy of state law, and depends upon** it for its stability, no less than for its very existence.

Thus, then, the first principle we ascertain about Money is that, in addition to being currency, it is **a patent article made only by the State** (the law standing in relation to it as a patent does to ordinary manufactures), which the law makes use of as the **standard of value.**

'Money,' says Aristotle, 'hath its value only in virtue of law and hath it not by nature; hence an alteration of the consensus between them that use it, hath power to destroy the value which as money it possesseth to meet men's wants.'

The patentee's rights are *absolute* and *perpetual*, and as manufacturer, the State stands in the place of managing director of a company, of which the shareholders are the nation, their profits being derived, not from periodical dividends, but from the facilities afforded them in all transactions, whether public or private, by the use of **the patent article—Money.**

It is important to bear in mind, that the nation are the company who own the manufacturing rights, and one of the conditions under which production should be carried on — a clause imperatively necessary in the Articles of this company—is that any shareholder, *i.e.* every single member of the community possessing the raw material, **may demand** at the Mint its **equivalent** in the **manufactured** article, **Money.** That equivalent is fixed by law, and unless it exists, and exists, moreover, coincidently with free mintage, there can be no stability in the standard of value. In England, at present, any one owning an ounce of Gold can demand for it at the Mint, £3. 17s. 9d. But if his right to do so were withdrawn; if the Mint had power to refuse to deliver the Patent article in exchange for the raw material, the owner of it would find himself with a quantity of an ordinary commodity, possessing merely an uncertain and fluctuating value, for which a watchmaker might offer £3. 5s., and a jeweller £3. 12s.

The right of free mintage, therefore, at the fixed or legal equivalent, is essential to the stability of the standard of value.

It is in virtue of the right of free coinage at a fixed equivalent, that **the patentee, the State, controls the markets for the raw material,** out of which it manufactures Money, because by substituting a valueless thing, such as paper, for the precious metals, it can at once annihilate the main use to which they are put. It may cut off the demand for them, and thus lower their value; and, obviously, if the course adopted by one state were to be followed by a group of states, which gradually gained fresh adhesions, the limits of the fall which would occur in the value of the precious metals must be indefinite, checked only by the trifling demand which would be left for them as ornament, plate, &c., and even this would soon lose its former influence on values, because of their having already become shifting and doubtful. The mere beauty of Gold would go for little in times like these (when so-called 'aluminium' cannot be detected from the 'nobler' metal by the uninitiated), except it were that the demand *for Gold as Money* is steadily increasing, and its permanent and steady value supposed to be thus assured.

This permanent and steady value is the result of the consensus existing between those who use money; in other words, **the legal value is only another designation of the 'intrinsic' value.** The labour employed in the production of the raw material may be the better paid for, or the worse, but, as miners best of all men know, their remuneration is a question of chance (which, indeed, is the overpowering attraction for many), and is never considered in the price of gold. The speculative charms about mining are so great, that even when through 'ill luck' a working has been stopped, it is not long before fresh adventurers appear on the spot. The cost of a bag of sovereigns from California will be altogether different to that of a bag from Australia, though each contain one thousand coins, yet even Professor Bonamy Price would not expect the one bag to purchase more commodities than the other. A mine may turn out, one month, 1,000 ozs. of gold, upon which the month's expenses prove to be £3,887. 10s., in which event there will not be a penny of remuneration to the miner, because no one will give him more than the Mint equivalent per oz.—£3. 17s. 9d. Another month, a similar weight of gold may be raised at a cost of £500, when the miners' profit will be £3,387. 10s. 'There is my price,' says the buyer at the mine; 'the fixed standard value; it is no use for me to offer you less, for you could get the price elsewhere; it would be absurd for me to offer you more, because it would simply be loss to me.' If the buyer be a Moralist, he will frequently add, 'I am sorry the cost of production has been so heavy as to nearly ruin you, but you know the Mint will not give me the £6 per oz. which this gold has cost you.'

The most imaginative ideas on this part of the subject prevail among the theoretical financiers, and are clearly expressed by Professor Price. He thinks that 'those who determine the price to be paid at the mines, are the miners and the buyers of the gold together. The miners must have reward enough in the command of wealth given them, however calculated, to induce them to dig up the ore, and the buyers must see their way to selling the gold to purchasers who will leave them a profit on the purchase.' Our professor is not 'a practical man.' He may have read in his youth of the manner in which buying and selling at the mines was effected thirty years ago, when one hundred millions of our existing gold was being raised; if he has not, let him refer to a most charming book,* where he will find that in the days of 1850 the 'cost of production' never entered men's heads. If the 'knife and the revolver' had not already determined 'the price to be paid at the mines,' the gambling hells of San Francisco soon settled the question for the producer; as 'the ordinary miner, elated with success, suddenly possessed of unwonted wealth, staked his gold recklessly, unconscious that the professional gambler with keen eye was watching his prey.' Five years later—and perhaps this is where our professor has got confused—'the price at the mines' was determined by the miners' necessities for spirits, food, and clothes; but now, and in all settled conditions of mining, there is no room for the haggling and palaver which Mr. Price seems to think determines the price to be paid. There

* *Pioneering in the Far East*, Ludvig Verner Helms.

is no time lost between producer and buyer, the bank's agent being on the spot, ready with the fixed value, in sovereigns, of the raw material. As for the fancy sketch of the 'men who possess ingots of precious metal' solemnly discussing whether or not the Mint shall have their gold or whether they shall 'import it into England' to the alarm of the bank directors—it is a companion picture to 'The Lunatic Merchant' now in Professor Bonamy Price's collection, which shall be exhibited in a moment; the pair being suggestive of the celebrated gallery at Brussels, where your guide shrugs his shoulders and says, 'Very, very clever, you know, but quite mad.'

The Patentees can increase the supply of Money at their pleasure, as England did in 1666 by affording *free* mintage of Silver and Gold, or check the production of Money, as was done in 1816, by abandoning the coinage of pure Silver altogether, and substituting for it our existing debased and very limited token coinage. Our existing Silver currency is depreciated by alloy to the extent of about 8 per cent., and is legal tender in payment of debts only for the sum of 40s. The circulation of this token money does not exceed 10s. per head of the population.

So long as free mintage of Gold and Silver is maintained, there is no prospect of there being more Money than the world can absorb. Through the agency of steam and electricity, the distribution of Money over the globe can be effected almost instantaneously, so that there becomes less and less probability of a glut in one market, and scarcity in another. Professor Bonamy Price, however, is alarmed at the possibility of there being idle capital in the Bank, and the tableaux in which he exhibits his fears deserve a place 'on the line' along with the other effects of this master of finance.

Tableau I. shows 'a merchant' who has been doing rather a large cash business with Australia, and finds himself burdened with the proceeds of English goods to the extent of five million sovereigns. He is in the Antipodes, and finding that 'the currency is full at the time'—whatever that may mean—he decides on 'importing into England' this trifling sum of five millions sterling.

Tableau 2. The Gold has arrived. No one knew of its coming, for telegrams, both public and private, have, of course, been stopped. What is to be done with it? Will 'Rothschild take it off for abroad?' The city pauses for a reply. *Rothschild will not take it!* And it must be left idle and useless in the vaults of the Bank.

Tableau 3. 'An interior dimly lighted.' It is the Bank parlour, where round the table droop the forms of several men bewailing their fate It has been announced to the Directors of the Bank of England, that £5,000,000, in sovereigns, have arrived from Sydney, and are lying idle in the vaults.

If, in these pictures, Mr. Bonamy Price is exercising his wit upon the practical men whom he despises,—good and well; there is not the least objection—but if he is in earnest; if he really fancies that these tableaux depict the processes by which practical men carry on business, it is time he were taught that it is the merest folly to attempt to influence their minds, or the minds of any intelligent persons, with such imaginative nonsense. Mr. Price's 'merchant' is an imbecile who should be taken care of by his friends; at least, if he be not altogether imbecile, he should be condemned to teach theoretical finance for the rest of his natural life. The man did his country the service, at any rate, of leaving it; and, as his was a purely cash business, the five millions which he invested in English manufactures will have been circulating in his absence, to the benefit of English trade. But he must be simply mad, if he ships these five million sovereigns from Sydney to London without telegraphing to know whether or not they are wanted there. If 'Money is scarce,' he may send them with advantage, and profitably employ them; but, supposing Money to be abundant in London, he will (presuming him, for the moment, to be clothed and in his right mind) look at wool, or wheat, or copper, or tin, either for the home market or elsewhere. And even if the man being sane should miscalculate, or, being insane, should, without reason, 'import' these five million sovereigns into England, they would (if not immediately wanted on their arrival) very soon make their presence felt by stimulating trade and causing new demands for Money. Practical men know the strength given to every transaction by a large metallic reserve in the National Bank, and no one doubts that if these millions were available, and waiting investment, it would not be long before many a new industrial and speculative undertaking would be started. This effect would be produced even if Price & Co. kept their chests of Gold lying in the Bank vaults, but the probabilities are, that they would make another of their cash coups for Australia, and that their five millions would go circulating through the Provinces.

The State has the power, as has been seen, to destroy any coins falling short of the standard which it has arbitrarily fixed; and it may go further, and alter the standard itself, as it did in 1717, by declaring that a guinea, which had formerly been exchangeable for 21*s.* 6*d.*, should, in future, be paid and received as the equivalent of 21*s.*; or, again, as in 1816, when the guinea was ignored and the sovereign established by law as the sole standard of value. England has but seldom exercised these supreme powers, but in France, during one reign alone, the standard was altered so often, that it was said to be difficult to find a man who understood the currency at all.

Capricious interference with the standard of value must create uncertainty in all transactions based upon it, and the injurious effects will be the better understood by considering the results that would follow from any ill-judged legislation which were to change the standard of measure or capacity—the yard, or the universally reverenced pint—and hence we arrive at a second great principle regarding Money. That **stability is the desideratum in the standard,** and since the standard is the sole property of a patentee, it is just and reasonable that the maker should be called on to guarantee it to the fullest extent possible, against frequent and violent fluctuations.

Money, viewed as currency, that is to say, the one article which passes everywhere in exchange for commodities, will procure more or less of them according to its abundance or scarcity. When the patentees are busy, turning out a steady supply of their material, its exchangeable power will keep pretty much the same; but if from any cause a check arises in the supply of money, prices of all commodities become unsettled and decline, or, in other words, more of them have to be given in exchange for a fixed sum of Money; and thus, at the present time, every one is familiar with the fact that the buying power of Money (owing to a scarcity of the yellow material of which it is made, and to the restrictions put by law upon the use of the white) has increased.

But the standard of value must remain **untouched and unshaken,** if it is to be worth the name, and must continue thus distinguished from the varying amount of any given commodity which may happen to be measured by it.

By common consent, there are but two metals available as the standard of value—Gold and Silver. At one time of the world's history Gold has been the selected standard; at another, Silver. At a third, **both metals have been used,** a definite relative value between the two being determined by law.

Nations which have used **an amalgam of the two,** have been sometimes tempted to narrow their system. The huge discoveries of Silver by the Spaniards made Gold rise rapidly in the estimation of Europe. The unprecedented output of Gold from Australia and San Francisco, determined Holland to limit herself to a Silver standard. England, in 1816, abandoned her Bi-metallic standard of Gold and Silver for a single Gold one, but the superstition that she owes her commercial supremacy to thus stealing a march on the nations of Europe, and securing their Gold, was exposed by Mr. Disraeli in his speech at Glasgow, in 1873, when he said, **'Our gold standard is not the cause of our commercial prosperity, but the consequence of our commercial prosperity.'** It served our purpose so long as other nations chose to take our Silver from us, or to give us Silver at a fixed price, whichever we desired, but from the moment that our own policy was imitated by Germany, which, in 1873, followed England's example of 1816, and discarded Silver, this country has been suffering a loss which cannot be estimated. Nor has the country which imitated us been more fortunate than we. ' While the area of civilisation is widening,' writes Professor Thorold Rogers, and ' therefore the demand for an adequate currency is being extended, Germany has abandoned a Silver for a Gold currency, and has had, as a fruit of its successful war with France, an exceptional power of attracting Gold to itself, with singular success indeed, *but to the incredible misfortune of its people.*'

Here, then, are two instances of great nations narrowing their standard of value; two occasions on which the shareholders in great companies sacrificed their right to the free manufacture or mintage of their raw material, and in both cases history will echo Professor Rogers' words, that such a change was followed by 'bad times.' These two instances are typical and excellent as illustrations. England, in 1816, throwing out of use a large portion of her currency, restricts herself to a single Gold standard, and there ensued such a period of disaster, that Sismondi could say of it, in 1827, 'It is five years since the suffering began; far from being allayed, it seems increasing with time.' And Sir James Graham declared regarding it, 'One class flourished, and that was triumphant—the class of annuitants—and the tax-eater rejoiced in the increased value of money, in the sacrifice of productive industry to unproductive wealth, *in the victory of the drones over the bees.*'

A remembrance of one of the first principles we have already derived from our study will enable us to account for these disasters, and to see that they were inevitable, viz. **that any country which constructs its standard of value, upon one half only of the available precious metals rather than upon the amalgamated whole, thereby exposes itself to perturbations** which must follow the sudden and enforced action of the patentee who ceases to produce, or is obliged greatly to check production for want of the raw material. Suppose the production of Bessemer steel to be suddenly cut off one half, through the failure of one of the two kinds of iron which, for the sake of example, we will assume to be used in its manufacture, and what would be the disorganisation of the trade dependent on it?

The losses arising from the immediate convulsion of prices would be bad enough, but the direst misfortune would come out of *the uncertainty* as to the future of values, and *distrust in their stability*.

It was a shock of this nature which was given to the stability of the monetary standard by the German Government, in the year 1873, and the extent of it is but feebly gathered from the foregoing illustration. For it is a shock of which the world has only *as yet felt the first effects*, but which are intensifying, if we accept the judgment of a court to which appeal shall be made in a moment.

England, in 1816, be it remembered, discarding Silver, drained the continent of Gold at a cost of several millions to herself, but she fortunately failed to produce monetary chaos, *because* there were silver-using states open to buy her Silver. Germany discarded Silver in 1873, and the Latin union was forced to cease coining it, **and monetary chaos is threatened,** just because there are no states to buy; because other nations took the alarm; because, in short, suspicion of Germany's intentions created a panic among the users of Silver, and everybody lost faith in its *stability*. The countries which had based their values on an amalgamated Gold and Silver standard, declined to carry out the mistaken policy of Germany. The confederate states which had legalised the free coinage of both metals, ordered its cessation in self-defence, and, as the result, the mean value per ounce which Silver had maintained for seventy years fell twenty per cent., with the prospect of a further and an indefinite decline. In a word, to speak roughly, and in round figures, one half of the Money used for the world's transactions has been to this extent depreciated, and is threatened with expulsion from the rôle it had hitherto maintained, as joint base of the standard of values among the nations of the world. It is as if some supreme authority in London had entirely stopped the omnibus traffic and restricted locomotion to hansom cabs.

And thus has arisen what is called '**The Silver Question**,' which is this : shall the uncertainty as to the future continue, or can measures be adopted which will restore Silver to the position it formerly held as Legal Tender, and shall the precious amalgam—Gold and Silver—be made the International Standard of Value?

Shall half the world's Money be thrown out of use? That is the plainest, most practical way, perhaps, of putting '**The Silver Question**.' The world is computed to be using fifteen hundred millions sterling of Silver and Gold, and her business expands at a gigantic pace. Shall she discard 700 millions of Silver? Shall she abandon (to use the words of Mr. W. Bagehot) 'the normal currency (silver) which is suited to those small transactions which constitute the bulk of the dealings of mankind?'

Am I thought to be overstating the case? Let us see. The International Conference held in Paris, in 1867, looked forward with confidence to a continuance of the Gold supply, the American delegate putting it down as an addition to the world's stock for 'many successive periods of fifteen years' of an amount equivalent to 26 millions sterling per annum, with the 'possibility of a still more enormous production.' A single Gold standard for Europe and America was therefore thought to be practicable.

A beautiful dream! It had been rudely broken in upon when the next Conference met in Paris, composed of sadder and wiser men. The annual production of Gold for the ten years had proved to be 19 in place of 26 millions, as the theorists said *it ought to have been*. Germany, without saying 'by your leave,' and with a mystery dear to Prince Bismarck, had begun to throw away her Silver, the fall in which had become so alarming that a Committee of the House of Commons, with Mr. Goschen as Chairman, had been set to inquire into the depreciation, which had already inflicted heavy loss upon the British empire. The following was one of their general conclusions :—

'If effect should be given to the policy of substituting Gold for Silver, wherever it is feasible .... and thus displacing Silver from the position it has always occupied, of doing the work of the currency over at least as large an area as Gold, **no possible limit could be assigned to the further fall in its value which would inevitably take place.**'

In 1878 the second Conference assembled in Paris, and their decision is confirmatory of the opinion of the English Committee, and suggests a mode of escape from the disasters which were foreseen.

'**It is necessary to maintain in the world**

the monetary functions of Silver as well as of Gold, but the selection for use of one or other of the two metals, or of both simultaneously, should be governed by the special position of each state or group of states.'

Some words from Mr. Goschen, one of the delegates of England, are most important as helping to establish us in another step to a just conclusion. He said, 'the Indian Government had suffered great loss; the merchants had suffered from fluctuations in value, and public functionaries had suffered from the depreciation, but England has given proof of her faith in regard to Silver, by waiting to see whether it would not recover its former value. Had the example of other countries been followed in India, and precautions taken by limiting the mintage or introducing Gold, Silver might have fallen an additional ten or fifteen per cent. If, however, other states were to carry on a propaganda in favour of a Gold standard and of the demonetisation of Silver, *the Indian Government would be obliged to reconsider its position, and might be forced to take measures similar to those taken elsewhere,*' *i.e.* discard Silver.

That these words were spoken not as a mere threat, but under a sense of a possible imperious necessity, is clear by a comparison of them with the declaration of the Indian representative in the present Conference, 'It is certain that if the depreciation of Silver continues, and . . . if the opportunity should offer itself, we should be only too ready to seize it and return to the proposals of the Commission which sat at Calcutta in 1868, and to enter, though much against our will, into **the struggle which is about to commence between the nations of the earth, for the sole metal which will be left to us as the solid basis of an international currency.**'

The Conference of 1878 broke up, leaving the commerce of the world in an admittedly woeful plight; with 'prices, profits, and wages falling,' stagnation at home and trade with foreign countries harassed by the uncertainties attaching to the monetary standard.

Between the Gold-using portion of the world and the Silver-, business had become more the work of a gambler than a merchant, for commodities were being measured by a standard which shifted with the caprice of an English climate. In one year the ratio between Gold and Silver, which opened at 1 to 16·10, sprang to 1 to 19·4 within a period of six months, and fell in as short a succeeding space to 1 to 16·50. With such a wildly fluctuating standard as this, the commerce of Europe, estimated at £2,000,000,000, was left to 'flounder and founder.' English exports, although the same in quantity, fell within four years 20 per cent. in value, with a result to manufacturers, which is hinted at in Mr. Giffen's statement, thus —'*profits depend upon price*, and this is an especially important consideration, in the foreign export trade.' The figures of the cotton trade may be adduced as an illustration of what was happening. In 1873 Lancashire had exported 214 million pounds of yarn, and valued it at £17,000,000, in 1877 the export was 227 millions, and the value only £12,000,000. Of manufactured cottons there had been shipped, in 1873, 3·50 billion yards, valued at £56,000,000, while in 1877 the quantity, which had increased by about 3 million yards, had fallen in value to £51,000,000. In a word, the shrinkage in value on this one portion of the world's industries was about £17,000,000.

Was it any wonder? These exports be it remembered, or at least the bulk of them, were going to be paid for in Silver money, *but the world was beginning to have a horrible suspicion that its silver was 'bad.'* Liverpool and London made formal representations to the Government. Lord Beaconsfield publicly called attention to the serious state of affairs, thus: 'While the produce of the Gold mines has been steadily diminishing, while these great alterations in favour of a Gold standard have been made, notwithstanding an increase of population, which alone *requires always* a considerable increase of gold currency to carry on its transactions, the amount every year has diminished—Gold is every day appreciating in value, and as it appreciates in value the lower become the prices.'

Among the official statements of the late Government, was the assurance that **the 'Silver Question'** was having consideration.

Last year, for the third time, an International Conference met in Paris to attempt a settlement of the question. On its decision hang momentous interests. There can be no question that it is so, for let us now appeal to the Court, to which reference has already been made, and whose judgment will command general respect.

Mr. Goschen, as the Chairman of the Parliamentary Committee of 1876, had agreed that a further displacement of Silver would lead to an indefinite fall in its value; and Mr. Walter Bagehot, a witness before that Committee, had affirmed, that the fall then already caused by the legislation of 1873 must injuriously affect the exports of manufactured goods from England to all Silver-using countries. At the Conference of 1878, with the fact before him, that the danger which had presented itself to his mind in '76 was coming nearer, Mr. Goschen asserted that '**The scramble to get rid of silver might provoke one of the gravest crises ever undergone by commerce;**' and that 'if all States should resolve on the adoption of a Gold standard the question arose—Would there be sufficient Gold for the purpose, *without a tremendous crisis?* There would be a fear, on the one hand, of a depreciation of Silver, and one, on the other, of a rise in the value of

Gold and a corresponding fall in the prices of all commodities. Again, there was a further important question. Italy, Russia, and Austria, whenever they resumed specie payments, would require metal; and if all other states went in the direction of a Gold standard, these countries too would be forced to take Gold.'

Already this **scramble for Gold,** which is the necessary and inevitable result of the abandonment of Silver, and which Mr. Goschen foresaw, has commenced. Italy has resolved to resume specie payments, and, afraid to take the discredited metal, Silver, is raising a Gold loan, thus withdrawing many millions sterling from the circulation of other nations—not from a preference for Gold, but, as was said by her delegate at the Paris Conference, '*from necessity.*' 'Because,' he added, ' she sees Silver depreciated by the suspension of coinage in the Latin union; by the Gold Mono-metallic legislation of Germany because she is obliged by the most elementary prudence not to expose herself to serve as a reservoir of debased metal, and, as the Finance Minister said in the Italian Parliament, to become *the monetary India of Europe.*'

Still more startling is the resolve of the President of the United States, to recommend to Congress the cessation of Silver coinage and a consequent increased use of Gold. Even with the help of a Silver currency, the States have taken from Europe 60 millions of Gold within the last few years, and the magic-like growth of the great cities in the west, is absorbing an amount of metallic currency which increases every year, and is likely to assume colossal proportions. When Austria and Russia resume specie payments, are they likely to be satisfied with the leavings of Europe and America? Why cannot the United States use their own Silver? why would not Italy adopt it? why will not France go back to her Bi-metallic standard and coin

A Plain Statement.

Gold and Silver equally for all comers at a fixed ratio? why cannot the entire bulk of the world's money be once more placed at the world's disposal for the furtherance of international trade? why cannot **stability** be thus imparted to values of all kinds?

Simply because England, posing as the Pecksniff of creation, prefers to say, 'We thank you, we are grateful to you with our whole heart. It is a blessed distinction that you have conferred upon us—this of a Gold standard; believe us, we shall not easily forget it.' Because this country, which from the universality of her commerce, if for no better reason, might have been expected to have outgrown insular prejudices, does not as yet comprehend that the heavy Gold chain which adorns the Pecksniffian waistcoat, *is a mere consequence of prosperity, and not its cause.*

Mr. Pecksniff was represented at the Paris Conference of 1878. 'Mr. Pecksniff said grace, a short and pious grace, invoking a blessing on the appetites of those present; and committing all persons who had no Gold to the care of Providence, whose business (so said the grace in effect) it clearly was to look after them. Perhaps there never was a more moral man than Mr. Pecksniff, especially in his conversation and correspondence. It was once said of him by a homely admirer, that he had a Fortunatus's purse of good sentiments in his inside. In this particular he was like the girl in the fairy tale, except that if they were not actual diamonds which fell from his lips, they were the very brightest paste and shone prodigiously. He was a most exemplary man; fuller of virtuous precepts than a copy book. Some people likened him to a direction post, which is always telling the way to a place, and never going there.'

Such is the distinguished rôle which England has been filling.

It may be taken on the highest authority that the scramble for Gold has begun. And now to enable us to judge the better of its probable results, we will cite the opinion of a second member of the Court, admittedly one of the first statisticians of the day, Mr. Robt. Giffen. Writing in 1879, he calls attention to the fact that for twenty years the average production of Gold had fallen from thirty to twenty millions per annum, while at the same time estimating that the growing demands of the world had increased to about twenty-seven millions. The following is his conclusion :—

'If the scarcity of Gold has as yet contributed very little to our money troubles, or the fall in prices, **it must at least be about to have that effect if no great change comes.**' Seeing no relief which can be looked for, from new banking or financial expedients, Mr. Giffen adds the following significant words :—

'**It would be nothing short of calamitous to business if another demand for gold, like the recent demands for Germany and the**

United States, were now to spring up. Even a much less demand would prove rather a serious affair before a very long time elapsed.'

The third member of our Court of Appeal, the late Baron Rothschild, confirms the opinion of the statesman and the statistician, in these words: '**The suppression of silver would amount to a veritable destruction of values, without any compensation.**'

This unanimous and weighty judgment is accepted by the theoretical financiers headed by Professor Bonamy Price, who in his last essay concedes that ' a coinage composed of Gold solely would be loaded with mischief, present and future. There is not, and almost certainly there never will be, Gold enough to do itself alone the work of money needed by all civilised nations. Hence, fluctuation in its value might be most frequent and most violent, and from such a source, complications and misfortunes, endless in number and intense in kind, might easily arise.'

A Plain Statement.

The scarcity of Gold is now, without a shadow of doubt, causing Money troubles. The demand from Italy must be met. The United States rapidly increase their absorption of Gold as the new cities of the west spring into being, and a huge population cry out for the only stable currency left to the world. The reserve of the Bank of England diminishes year by year, while the strain on it, arising from the demands of commerce, becomes heavier, and yet the men are called pessimists who venture to point to the inevitable outcome of it all—an outcome foretold by Mr. Goschen, Baron Rothschild, and Mr. Giffen, and accepted as inevitable by Professor Bonamy Price—an outcome which will be similar in character to the fate which befalls every man of business who trades too greatly in excess of *his immediately available capital.*

It is idle to appeal to the growth of manufactories and houses, to the increase of shipping &c. All these are an enormous addition to the nation's wealth, but they stand for so much *locked-up capital*; productive, it is true, but *not realisable*, and it is realisable securities that a nation, just as much as a banker, ought to hold in proportion to his business. Without them we know what happens if a 'Black Friday' comes.

The commercial interests of the country cannot be separated from the interests of *labour*. Throw away one half of the world's metallic currency, and the balance doubles its power as the equivalent for commodities. But if bread should fall to fourpence per quartern, will the workman eat more of it, or be satisfied with a reduction of his wages from thirty shillings a week to fifteen? Yet says Mr. Giffen, 'it is incredible that the great change should occur *without the labourer being affected*,' or, in plain English, without a dismal succession of strikes, failure, and ruin.

Is it then going beyond the truth to affirm that 'The Silver Question' affects every class in the country—capitalist and artisan, landowner and labourer?

Is there any way out of the wood?

The voices that cried 'Peace, peace' are dying out of hearing, and almost any finance article taken at random from the daily press evidences the uneasiness felt at the prospect of the '*scramble for Gold.*'

Gold Mono-metallism (summarising in that term the views of the Paris Conference in 1867) has been slowly vanishing from sight, and, like Alice's cat in Wonderland, has left nothing of itself but the *grin*. The advocates of the single Gold standard, alarmed at the 'scramble' in which they may be overturned, admit the gravity of the situation, and have their own way of meeting it. They assign the yellow metal to one group of countries and the white to another, arguing that by this means the needful outlet for Silver will be found, the precious metals will be fairly divided, and a relative ratio between them maintained. This solution of the difficulty, they tell us, is simply and easily applied—Gold for the rich nations, Silver for the poor relations. Over the doors of the smaller countries of Europe and, presumably, over America, a notice is to be affixed —'**Silver may be shot here.**'

Let the value of this proposal be tested by suggesting to the private bankers of England, that they should store the Silver in the country, and leave the Gold to the joint-stock institutions. Is it credible that nations, any more than individual merchants or bankers, will arrange themselves in clusters marked rich and poor, to meet the wishes of the Gold standard advocates? Can it be conceived that any single country will step forward and say, 'I will be the charity boy, dress me in your white small-clothes'? Mr. Goschen had Italy in his eye, and so had Mr. Giffen, when they were arranging their distribution of Silver, but Italy has demanded the uniform of the big boys. Holland was present in their minds, without doubt, as one of the rubbish heaps where Silver might be thrown; but Holland is already bracing herself to face the loss which must follow the demonetisation of Silver that will be forced upon her. The United States have declared against the white metal, so long as it is tabooed by Europe, and, by way of emphasising their determination, have been for some time past drawing from her an amount of Gold equal to the entire annual production.

Where is the Silver to be taken? How shall it be got rid of? Surely the British Empire should insist upon an answer, for she holds half the stock of Silver in the world. The smaller nations of Europe, having declined it, is it likely that France or Austria or Russia will be satisfied to hold it?

'Happy thought,' *send it to India;* and there are to be found persons, who imagine that by drenching one part of the empire with a metal discarded as Money by the entire west, you will *benefit the natives.* The fall in the value of the rupee from 2s. to 1s. 8d. is regarded by this *Exeter Hall* clique of financiers as so distinctly in the interest of the 'mild Hindoo,' that they can calmly contemplate its further indefinite fall, perhaps to 6d., by which time it may be hoped that the welfare of India will be assured, and its grand consummation of happiness arrived at; because it must be clear that this fancied enrichment of the people of India can be brought about only at the expense of the British manufacturer and consumer. While the Silver coin of India is falling, prices of native produce *will tend to rise,* and the increased cost must fall upon the European, who has ultimately to meet it in *Gold*; and at the same time the prices paid in India for

British manufactures *will tend to fall*, and the Lancashire weavers will have to be content with lower prices for calicoes. Manchester is beginning to comprehend this.

It is sufficient to remark, that just as the **stability of the value of Silver is shaken**, so the natives of India will come, like everybody else, to care little or nothing for a metal which —like a false friend—is one thing to-day, and another to-morrow.

As to the trade of this country with the East, let me quote from the speech of Sir Louis Mallet (Under Secretary of State for India). 'During the last few years I have had too many proofs that the interests of trade have been seriously affected and injured in consequence of the depreciation (of Silver) to doubt the reality of the losses incurred. It is, no doubt, true, that when trade has been able to adapt itself to an alteration in the relative value of the standards of the two countries, *if this* alteration were of a permanent character, and took place once for all, the evil would cease. But this is not the case. The future is as uncertain as the present in the existing state of things, and it is this uncertainty which impedes and prevents trade.'

'Happy thought,' the 'Heathen Chinee!' he would accept the abandoned seven hundred millions of Silver money from Europe, with 'a smile that was childlike and bland.' But *what will he give us in exchange?*

Let me re-state the judgment of the Court against whose decision no appeal will be lodged.

Commerce is drifting into a 'calamitous' condition; towards 'a destruction of values without any compensation.' The danger consists in **'the scramble for Gold'** and the general demonetisation of Silver. The court is agreed about this, and it has been shown that the danger is nearing us. One of our professed guides, the exclusively Gold standard advocate has disappeared. A second, who fully admits the gravity of the situation, offers us directions which are found to be hopelessly impracticable. We are left asking :—

'Is there any way out of the wood?'

The Bi-metallists, those who advocate a combination of the two precious metals, as the standard of value, speak with hope and confidence, and there is this at least which may predispose us to place faith in them, viz. that, in season and out of season, they have been, for the last seven years, denouncing the step taken by Germany in 1873, and foretelling with exactness the course of events and gradual approach of the danger with which we are now confessedly face to face.

Their advice is, at any rate, intelligible, and based upon the great first principles which have been elicited from this brief inquiry.

'Up to 1873,' so we may imagine the Bi-metallists saying, 'you were living in a fools' paradise. You thought that your boasted Gold Currency was **the cause**, instead of **a mere consequence of** your **wealth**; but during the past thirty years, the nations of Europe have been growing in commercial importance until, in 1873, Germany, befooled by the sudden and enormous gains wrung from her neighbour, decreed that a Gold coinage should be, what it has been with you, a *consequence* of prosperity. Sixty millions of Silver was thrown by her upon the market, and a like quantity of Gold purchased, thus making a new and unexpected drain on the supplies of the world's money to the extent of 120 millions sterling. The effect was instantaneous. It was not merely that Germany was, so to speak, throwing away sixty millions of Silver, but that she held *in terrorem* over Europe, a further indefinite quantity, with which she was prepared to deal in similar fashion at the first available opportunity. She exercised the power of law to drive out Silver money, and, by destroying the demand for the metal, at once depreciated its value. The countries which, by their joint dealing in Gold and Silver at a fixed ratio, had maintained the equilibrium, now took alarm and **put a stop to the free coinage of silver.** Faster and faster, therefore, extended the distrust in its future; more and more eager became the desire to secure the only metal which possessed stability, and of which supplies were yearly diminishing.

'The **stability** of Silver has been thus incontrovertibly overthrown by mistaken legislation. The Gold deluge of 1850 poured over Europe, yet only in one country did panic go so far as to demonetise Gold. Ten Comstock lodes might have been discovered, and no harm been done, if one of the great states had not forced the demonetisation of Silver upon Europe. Your suspicions that half the world's money is "bad" are not without foundation, for one nation after another is being compelled to cast it away, and thus **"the scramble for Gold"** has been brought about, and must become more fast and furious as time goes on. The law which *made* Silver an integral part of the standard of value has, for the moment, dissolved the partnership between Gold and Silver, and we maintain that it was a blunder to do so, **but the law can resettle the partnership on the old basis.** Law gave a fixed value to Silver by introducing the demand for it as *Money*, and Law can restore that value by resuming the use of Silver. The patentees who manufacture *Money*, and have the sole right to utilise it as the standard of value, have before now employed *both Gold and Silver*, and if they please they can do so again. The moment that Silver is decreed to be once more legal tender, that moment, the column on which the world's commerce has rested—a metal column amalgamated of Gold and Silver—will be restored and the standard of values will be based **on the two metals, on the whole available metallic currency, instead of on one half of it.** Discoveries of one alone of the precious metals cannot then disturb stability, for the new volume, whether of the yellow stream or the white, will be quietly absorbed in the ocean of the world's currency. With *two* reservoirs connected together from which commerce can draw, the supply must be more certain and unfailing than with one, and it is just these qualities—certainty and steady supply—which make up the desideratum in the standard, and which Mono-metallists, no less than ourselves, desire to attain, viz. **stability.** The supply to one reservoir may be short and the other overflowing, but since the contents of both will be distributed over the world, through *one and the same channel*, in one and the same form—**legal tender money** —Commerce, and the transactions of nations, and of private life, will alike enjoy those facilities which are an absolute necessity for the safe and undisturbed conduct of business.

Whether, for the moment, the Gold stream flow more freely, or the Silver, can make no difference. Neither one can advantage the individual or the nation more than the other, because so long as the main and absorbing demand for them comes from all civilized states of the world, so long must values remain fixed and unaltered, and the metals will, therefore, be always interchangeable, in a definite ratio, the one for the other. For **law, which creates the use, and fixes the value of both metals; law, which can change that value by abolishing the demand for them, can assuredly perform the lesser task of assigning a relative and an interchangeable value to each.** *There is no room for doubting the power of law to do this, for it has done so already.* From 1801 to 1873 the mean ratio between Gold and Silver was, as nearly as possible, 1 to 15½,* the ratio being maintained in the face of the most extreme fluctuations possible in the supplies of Gold. In a group of European States, called the Latin Union, the two sources—Gold and Silver—supplied one stream for years, in varying quantities, though in a fixed relation of value; to the prosperity of the Union, and the admitted advantage of Great Britain. '*As fifteen and a half is to one,*" said the Union, *basing the proportion not on caprice but on ascertained data,* " *so shall Silver be to Gold ;* " and the decree of four nations established this proportion for the world, to the world's immense comfort and convenience.

'And now, to the question, **"What shall be done with Silver?"** we answer—The road is plain, because **the world is waiting for the very article which is being wasted.** Only let the patentee recommence manufacture;

* See Table, p. 96.

only let law recreate the demand for Silver as legal tender money, and its stability is secure. And if one small group of nations had the power to maintain the relative exchangeability of Gold and Silver, how much more will the joint Powers of Europe and the United States succeed in doing so. The position of the precious metals will indeed have been made impregnable.

'The issue between us and the advocates of an exclusively Gold standard is a plain, intelligible one. The consequence of their doctrine is uncertainty in the present and distrust in the future. On all hands it is admitted, that while the area of commerce is extending, the metallic currency is being diminished. Any quantity of Gold taken from the Bank at once excites alarm and anxiety, and **at any moment the trade of the country, however sound, may be harassed or paralysed.** Our opponents' scheme for averting the danger is futile and absurd, because no nation, or group of nations, will use Silver at their bidding. *But the use for Silver must be found*, if International commerce is to be safe and progressive; and we maintain that it needs only the establishment of an International agreement, to create an outlet for all available Silver as legal tender money, by establishing it an integral part of the standard of value.

'The Mono-metallists' contrivance for preventing the threatened disasters (apportioning the Gold to the rich, and the Silver to the poor) is impracticable. And so also, spite of its distinguished advocacy, is an alternative scheme Professor Bonamy Price has at last accepted the necessity of re-establishing the free mintage of Silver at a fixed ratio to Gold, but propounds a method of his own. Gold, according to him, is to be the sole standard of value: Silver, an ordinary commodity, although unlimited legal tender, of which *the* ratio to gold is to be fixed from time to time by a competent authority, after a study of the bullion market. If Bi-metallism were adopted, the bullion market would not and could not show divergence from the value of money, but, on Mr. Price's plan, the Silver market will be the shuttlecock of speculators, open to the influence of every forged telegram, the sport of any designing operator, and the main advantage sought for by the remonetisation of Silver, viz. *the stability of the standard of value, will be sacrificed.* Mr. Price complains that we ignore the existing market ratio, which is 18 to 1, in favour of 15.50. But he must know very well that the difference has been brought about by the very policy he now recommends; through *the action of Germany in relegating Silver to the ordinary market for commodities*, and that the moment a Bi-metallic union is carried out, the ratio will return to 15.50 to 1. Practical men may be very confused, but they will assuredly, when they adopt Bi-metallism, select the stable form of it, rather than this *Bastard Bi-metallism* to which the Professor is standing sponsor. The re-establishment of the old system, when it comes, will be the work of statesmen, not of theorists, and the ratio will be restored without any of those excessive hardships which Mr. Price conjures up. That the change will not be effected without some inconvenience may be admitted, but it will be **the Drones that will suffer, not the Bees.**'

I have endeavoured to present the case of the Bi-metallists in a commonplace manner. I pretend to no originality, but have striven to make myself intelligible to persons who have not leisure for a lengthened study of the question, or the courage to face what they fancy to be a dry collection of literature on the subject. My belief is, that never was there a more urgent or momentous question before the country. Bi-metallism is not put forth as the cure for small-pox, nor is it expected to stamp out the cattle-disease; but it is at the very root of our commercial interests. It will, if true in principle, benefit agriculture, no less than commerce, for, as Mr. Gladstone lately remarked, it is *bad trade*, no less than bad weather, from which the farmers have suffered; and one main cause of bad trade is the uncertainties which cluster round the standard of monetary values, and the consequent diminution of the means by which the world's business is carried on. Take any one of the selected types of Money. Is it the wings of commerce? One wing has been cut off, and yet complaint is made that the bird will not fly. Is it the vehicle in which commerce is conveyed? One wheel is off, and yet we grumble that the chariot drives heavily. Is it the breath of commerce? The oxygen in it has been withdrawn, and is it matter for astonishment that the air becomes stifling?

The offer to assist in remedying all this is now made formally to England. It is not too much to say, that if she will join the union of civilised nations, the vexed question of currency may be settled, by the reconversion of the two precious metals into legal tender *Money*; and that Gold and Silver will again become the solid and stable standard of values for the civilised world.

There are grounds for hoping that this union may be realised. No one who studies the reports of the successive Monetary Conferences in Paris can doubt that a public opinion in favour of a Bi-metallic system is growing. The time is at hand when leaders of political thought who have committed themselves to the statement that Gold Mono-metallism is a Utopia, will confess that their proposed adaptation of Bi-metallism—the distribution of the two metals among the rich and poor nations—is a Utopia also, and that the only practicable, as well as logical, conclusion is, to distribute Gold and Silver universally, under the sanction of International law, and with the relative fixity of value which law can alone decree and maintain.

The cohesion and organisation which have been lacking among the advocates of Bi-metallism have been supplied, and the 'Journal of the Institute of Bankers,' about as safe and cautious an exponent of financial opinion as is to be found in the country, admits that a thorough discussion of the question is inevitable and desirable. References to it in the press become more frequent and less hostile, if not more appreciative, as the superstition that a Gold coinage is the *cause* instead of the *consequence* of our commercial prosperity, is yielding to the conviction that, without sacrificing, or even invalidating, that Gold coinage, we may possess ourselves of a *real* Silver currency instead of a sham one; a coin that shall deserve the name of currency, because part of the standard of value, and available for International purposes.

All suspicion of party purpose, of class interest, of anything wild or revolutionary in finance about the new movement inaugurated, is taken away by the standing and variety of its leading adherents. All that is wanting is a complete apprehension of its objects and a fair discussion of its principles, because the wider and more searching the inquiry and criticism, the more manifest will it appear that the aim of Bimetallism is **the development of local and international trade in its freest and fullest extent,** and that the principle which it seeks to exhibit in action is 'the greatest happiness for the greatest number.'

Let me close with the words of Sir Louis Mallet at the Paris Conference, words worthy of an English statesman, and having in them the presage of coming victory:—

'What is our position? *The annual pro-*

duction of the two metals is already barely sufficient. It is then obvious that Gold alone would be still less sufficient, especially when we remember that there is already a sensible reduction in its annual production.

'On the other hand, the need of Money, especially if it were invested universally with the legal tender faculty, increases and will increase still more rapidly.

'There are countries which would wish to revert to a metallic currency, or which are already preparing for it—Italy, Austria, and Russia. There are others like Germany, Spain, and even the United States, which have not got the quantity generally recognised as necessary. There is the increase of population and of transactions, especially in those countries which produce Gold; in short, there is material and intellectual progress in all countries. Is it not reasonable to conclude from all this, that we should be wise to prepare ourselves for the future in store for us, and to discover, if possible an International Standard more extended and more durable for the development of the commerce of the world? . . . At all events, it is an effort which ought to be made in the general interest. We have heard of a national selfishness, which, from a certain point of view, may be regarded as a patriotic virtue; but, in the question in which we are occupied at this moment, it is incontestable that an enlightened national selfishness is identical with true international interest.

'In the name of my Government, then, I thank the two Governments (France and the United States) who have initiated proposals with such objects in view.'

PART II.

OBJECTIONS ANSWERED.

If I should have had the good fortune to interest the reader in the first part of this little book, I hope he may be induced to give consideration to the remaining few pages. In them I have endeavoured to set forth very briefly the leading popular objections to the adoption of the Bi-metallic system under the sanction of international agreement. My desire has been to state the case of our opponents with perfect fairness, and to meet their objections in a like spirit. There are some few difficulties raised of a more intricate and technical nature than can be satisfactorily dealt with in a popular treatise, but I am satisfied that not one of them would be considered by Mono-metallists as of importance, *supposing* the objections which are here enumerated to be overruled.

Bi-metallists have no desire to snatch a verdict at the hands of the public. The more freely their case is discussed and criticised, the greater will be their satisfaction, because of their conviction that, as a study of their principles widens, so will the triumph of those principles be assured.

1. The historical statements are questioned. England, so it is urged, though using Silver and Gold Money prior to 1816, had really been on the Gold standard for a hundred years previously.

Answer. The free coinage of Silver and its use as legal tender was established by the Act of 1666. When Lord Liverpool wrote his celebrated letter to the king in 1805 he admits that there was no denying that 'every one has a right to bring Gold and Silver to the Mint to be converted into coin.' And when he used the word 'standard' in reference to Gold, he used it in the sense of the principal and most important coin, not as the sole measure of values.

The Act making Gold and Silver a legal tender dates from 1666, and was confirmed by successive Sovereigns. It was made 'perpetual' in 1768, and was never repealed until 1816!

2. The success of Bi-metallism in France up to 1873 was an accident, and is to be ascribed to the large demands for Silver caused by payments to India for cotton. It was a bad system for France, and actually impoverished her.

Answer. The demand for these exceptional payments to India lasted for only three years out of the long period that the Bi-metallic compact existed. As to the effect upon France, it was stated by the French representatives at the

Conference that the system had been a most profitable one for their country. If it impoverished her, it is quite inexplicable to find her equal to a strain of 600 millions sterling in the German war, and afterwards remaining one of the most prosperous countries in Europe.

3. Any great advance in the value of Silver would at once cause an enormous increase in production, and as Silver is much more abundant than Gold, the world would be inundated with it.

Answer. That one metal is abundant and the other scarce is an unwarranted assumption; the two metals being in many places, if not in most, found together.* This scare about an unlimited output of Silver is merely a repetition of the scare in 1867 about an excessive production of Gold from Australia and San Francisco. The accidental discovery of abund-

---

* See Table, page 99.

ance of either one precious metal or the other *may cause alarm to the advocate of a single standard*, but does not touch the Bi-metallist with the standard composed of the two metals.

It must be pressed upon the objector, that his fears are *no answer* to the demand of the world to be shown a way out of its *existing financial difficulty*, which arises from the fact that the available Silver currency is threatened with 'a further and indefinite fall in value,' and that while that process is going on, the foundations of commerce must continue unstable. The remarks of M. Leon Say at the Conference of '78 put the case most aptly : ' From a commercial point of view, the existence of the mass of coined Silver which is there all ready, of which man is already master, which he holds under his hand, and can let go or hold back as he wishes, according to the course of events, *exercises an influence far more decisive than that of a mass of Silver which is not yet produced, and*

Objections Answered.

which does not arrive in the market except gradually—a little at a time.'

4. The less valuable metal will always be at a discount, do what you will. Gold will be drained away from us, and we shall be left with Silver.

Answer. The fallacy here is that one kind of legal tender *is* more valuable than another, which cannot be the case. When Gold and Silver have become by international law the equivalent of one another in a fixed ratio; when fifteen and a half ounces of the one in money is exchangeable for one ounce of the other, all the civilised world over; when the yellow and the white material **form one measure**; when a fixed proportion of the one will procure exactly the same amount of commodities as does a relative proportion of the second; why should any nation or individual hanker after the one colour rather than the other? When the Monometallists can show us that a yard of cloth measured by a wooden stick, is more valuable than the same cloth cut from a metal yard measure affixed to a counter, they may induce people to believe that their fears would be realised. Up till recently, one half of the world preferred Silver, and there is every probability that they would continue to do so, **when the stability of Silver was re-established.**

The dread of England being drenched by the waters of the Silver stream and drained of the Gold, cannot be justified on any reasonable ground. The balance of trade, it is said, between us and America, tending more and more to be in favour of the latter, she will insist on being paid in Gold; but with International Bi-metallism established, *she could do nothing of the sort*, because when Gold and Silver have become International legal tender, *it will be at the option of Great Britain to pay in whichever metal is the more convenient at the time.* And how is it possible that we can be inundated with Silver?

Our imports vastly exceed our exports; so that to any country, as well as to America, it will be in our power to discharge outstanding debts in Silver or Gold at our option. There is every reason to believe that the adoption of Bi-metallism by the civilised world would bring about *in a natural way*, what the Mono-metallists are hopelessly trying to *force* into existence, viz. a distribution of Gold and Silver Money among the nations of the earth, in some definite proportion to their respective wants and capacities. Mr. Bagehot asserts that Silver 'is suited to those small transactions which constitute the bulk of the dealings of mankind,' and the moment that Silver is granted the dignity of International legal tender, it will perform this its natural function, being always in most demand among nations and communities where 'small transactions' are the most numerous.

A 'drain of gold' for one quarter or another

cannot exist under the conditions of International Bi-metallism; for the cause of such a drain is the disinclination of nations to take Silver, owing to the instability of its value. That cause must often operate under a system of either Gold Mono-metallism or Professor Price's Bastard Bi-metallism; for in each, Silver is a mere market commodity, and will never be accepted as unlimited legal tender. Nothing except the consensus of civilised nations can restore Silver to this position, and in doing so put an end to drains of Gold.

5. 'Bi-metallism is *unscientific.*' The objection is formidable, because so vague a one. What our opponents mean by it they would probably find it difficult to define. It is often 'unscientific' to be in opposition to received views. Galileo was very nearly burnt for being 'unscientific.' Columbus was called a fool and 'unscientific' for crediting the existence of a western continent. But, judging from the

writings of Mono-metallists, it would appear that our offence against science lies in teaching that a definite ratio can be maintained between two metals so unequally distributed as Gold and Silver, and that we are at variance with the law of demand and supply.

Answer. It was found that **it was the law which created the demand for the precious metals, because using them in the manufacture of the Patent article, Money.** Directly the State demand ceased, values fell, and if nations unitedly were to forswear the use of Gold and Silver as Money, the small outside demand for them for other purposes would not, and could not, prevent their falling indefinitely in value. **If the law can make the demand for and assign the value to one metal, it can do so in the case of both, and it may adopt what relation between them it chooses as most convenient.** On this aspect of the question Sir Louis Mallet thus expressed himself at the Conference: 'As regards the scientific basis on which Bi-metallism is founded . . . I may be allowed to express my unqualified dissent from the opinion that it is opposed to economic laws. I am disposed to think, on the contrary, that, considered as a whole, and with the conditions essential to its success (*i.e.* its general adoption and guarantee by International law), the Bi-metallic theory is in entire conformity with those great economic laws, which must always control the acts of the legislator and the fate of nations, and will continue to do so more and more; and that the idea which inspires it, is one of the most important and fruitful truths of science. . . . It is said That it is neither within the right nor the power of the legislator to regulate relative values of Gold and Silver. But how can such a proposition be maintained as regards the right? How can it be pretended that we have the right to impose on the population a single metal as Money, whether trade prefers another or not; and that we have not the right to give it the chance of using the two metals in fixed proportions, if such a course would be to its interest? As regards the power, can it be admitted that we can give an arbitrary, or, if you please, a conventional value to Gold or Silver, and yet that there is no power to fix their relation to each other?'

But apart from this, the distribution of the precious metals is extremely interesting to notice.

Sir Roderick Murchison speaks of it thus:—

'The quantities of Gold and Silver procurable will prove no more than sufficient to meet the exigencies of an enormously increased population, and an augmenting commerce and industry. Providence seems to have originally adjusted the relative values of the precious metals, and the **fact that their relations have remained the same for ages, will survive all theories.**'

Figures certainly support this view, for it is remarkable that, after one thousand years, the world's metallic wealth should be estimated as consisting of nearly equal proportions of Gold and Silver. But the result will be less surprising when it is remembered how often, nay, how generally, the two metals are found in connection with each other. In the two most productive mines in America, the Comstock and the Consolidated Virginia, the output has been 45 per cent. of Gold, and 55 per cent. of Silver,* while America's total production for the nine years ending 1879 showed an excess of Gold over Silver of £4,000,000.

The relative distribution of the precious metals is, however, no part of the argument for Bi-metallism, which rests upon human law, and not upon the acts of Providence.

The scare about an over-production of Silver is as difficult to allay as is the panic of

* The proportion of Gold was higher last year. See p. 98.

children who have been frightened with ghost stories. But the condition of mind is surely unworthy of men of business and judgment, and there are considerations which, fairly looked at, should tend to reassure them.

(*a*) The utter collapse of the prognostications at the Conference of '67 about Gold. The production had been 36 millions sterling per annum, and it was to maintain this average, even if it did not 'enormously' exceed it. Since the prophecy was uttered, and although Gold has been steadily appreciating in value, and therefore, according to the theorists, *ought* to have come forward in larger quantities, the supplies have been steadily diminishing, till we are avowedly in a condition of peril for the lack of them. From an annual production of 36 millions we have come down to just half the quantity.

(*b*) The similar falsity of the assurances made by *the Scarists* only a few years since, about the enormous production of the Comstock lode of Silver.*

(c) Granted that there will be occasional developments of production in both Gold and Silver, what reasons are there for fearing a convulsion in markets as the consequence? In the three years 1849 to 1851 the supply of Gold aggregated 26 millions. In the succeeding period the quantity was 92 millions sterling. Was the effect on the world's trade stimulating or depressing? And if, forty years ago, an annual production of nine millions of Gold could be followed, and followed with advantage, by an average output of 30 millions, is there any sufficient cause to dread even a greater increase now—if it should happen—when the world's commerce has so enormously increased and the necessity for metallic currency is correspondingly enlarged?

6. 'Mankind will not give up the use of

* See page 98.

Gold; as for every purpose of life, it is intrinsically the better metal, whether as a coin, or as a means of hoarding, or for use in the fine arts. It will eventually fetch the price which is necessary to keep up the supply, and if that price is fixed by law, an additional price or premium will be paid by the public. Bi-metallists have proved nothing, unless they can prove that, under the entirely new conditions they wish to create, the production of Gold will be sufficient, and the production of Silver will not be in excess of the public wants. Nothing seems more certain than that if Silver is produced in larger quantities than needed, it must, under the new system, force out Gold, and go on forcing it out till the quantity left is too small for the general wants of mankind, and at that moment Gold will command a premium in spite of the law.'

I quote the foregoing *in extenso*, because it is the view gravely expressed, after much thought and deliberation, by an able Monometallist.

Answer. (*a*) *Silver* has been and is preferred by half the world for coin and hoarding.

(*b*) The value of Gold and Silver used for manufacturing purposes is returned as about equal.

(*c*) To charge Bi-metallists with seeking to introduce 'new conditions' is *begging the question*. We assert, and challenge disproof of the statement, that under *the old Bi-metallic conditions* the price of Silver in relation to Gold varied only to a *fractional extent*, Mr. Baring, when examined before the House of Commons in 1828, estimating the variation in France as 'seldom above one-tenth per cent.' Since the destruction of the Bi-metallic compact, consequent on the action of Germany, the relative value of Silver **has never been steady**, and has fallen *twenty per cent.* from the highest point. *No* '*new conditions*' are demanded by Bi-metallists; they advocate a recurrence *to the old ones*, the fixity of which they would ensure by the wider guarantee of Europe and America.

(*d*) When Mono-metallists can forecast 'the wants of mankind' it will be time to call upon their opponents to 'prove that the production of Gold will be sufficient for and the production Silver will not be in excess' of those wants. To attempt either demonstration would be ridiculous. *At present*, there is no greater production of the *combined* precious metals than would be required for a general Bi-metallic currency; we can only hope that increased production may keep pace with the rapid extension of the world's needs.

(*e*) Mankind will insist on having their necessary supply of gold *at any price*! just as if the processes of mining and agriculture were identical, and it was only for mankind to offer 10s. per ounce more for the yellow metal to ensure the extra output, in the same way as you might ensure an increased acreage of cotton or sugar by raising the market price twenty per cent. Under a general system of Bi-metallism, it has been seen that (except in rare and unimportant cases) *Gold Money* can have no preference over Silver, and hence it must be in the mind of the objector, that mankind are prepared to pay any premium for the yellow metal, for the sake of hoarding it and for use in the fine arts.

(*f*) If, under the Bi-metallic International agreement, Silver (owing to the enormous output which it is gratuitously assumed will be realised, as soon as ever the metal regains its former value) is 'to force out gold,' and to 'go on forcing it out,' until there is too little left for the wants of mankind, **where is the 800 millions of the existing stock and the annual production, whether it be twelve or twenty millions, to be forced to?** This marvellous

Mono-metallic 'effect in black and white' shows us *one portion* of mankind 'forcing out' gold for no conceivable purpose, and *the other portion* determined to give any price for it, for no imaginable reason!

'The free concurrent circulation of the two metals in all countries,' says Mr. Baring, 'would certainly keep the proportions of each to the other most equable, and leave little other ground for fluctuation.'

7. Any International agreement come to for the concurrent use of Gold and Silver Money in a fixed ratio, even if practicable, which it is not, would be broken in case of war.

Answer. To the first clause of this favourite dogmatic assertion, so often and so loudly repeated that it has become wearisome, it can only be restated, at the risk of being equally tedious, that **the 'impossible' was a financial phenomenon witnessed in Europe for seventy years,** and it is a fair and logical deduction that if a small handful of states could keep up the equilibrium between Gold and Silver, **such an equilibrium might be made permanent by the combined action of Europe and the United States.**

War, even if a general one, could exert no injurious effect, for the obvious reason that each individual nation could only break the agreement at a tremendous loss to itself. How could it possibly help any country to depreciate the value of one-half of her metallic currency?

If the supposed breach of faith were a sudden one, the consequence must evidently be disastrous to the offending nation; if it were managed by a slow process extending over years, it could not at any rate fail to attract the notice of the world, and there would be time for the world to act on the defensive.

8. Gold would always be preferred to Silver for the settlement of International balances, because the charges for transport are so much

lighter. (This objection appeared recently in the City notes of a leading newspaper.)

Answer. The **charges for transport are the same.** £100,000 in Silver can be sent from London to Calcutta at the same charge as a like sum in Gold, *the freight being 'ad valorem.'*

9. The adoption of the Bi-metallic system in England would lead to great inconvenience among the banking interest, and in private life. We might be burdened with heavy payments *in Silver coin.*

Answer. Who is burdened *now* with heavy payments in Gold coin? although bankers might insist on paying a cheque for £5,000 in sovereigns. The bank note issued against the metallic reserve in the bank has relieved us of any inconvenience on this score, and it would perform exactly the same function in respect of Silver, when that had been decreed legal tender and constituted, therefore, a part of the bank reserve. The complaint in private life is of a *scarcity of Silver*, rather than of superabundance.

10. The attempt to remonetise Silver is the result of American diplomacy. The United States are the great producers, and they want to see higher prices for the metal.

Answer. The United States produce more Gold than Silver. and the Silver mines as well as the Gold are the property of private individuals and not of the Government, which has as much control over them as Mr. Gladstone has over the tin mines of Cornwall. The interest of the United States in **the Silver Question** is identical with the interest of Europe. They have a rapidly expanding trade abroad, and an unparalleled extension of commercial centres throughout their continent, all of which are absorbing currency and tend to absorb more. The United States share and freely express the fears which they entertain for their own commerce, consequent upon an insufficiency of Gold, and on this point, they are in entire accord with England, France, Germany, Austria, Italy, and Holland, as represented at the Paris Conference.

Date	Ratio	Supply Gold (£ Millions)	Supply Silver (£ Millions)	Proportion Gold to Silver. 1 to
1801–1810	15.61	2.6	7.7	2.97
1811–1820	15.51 ⎫	1.6	3.6	2.25
1821–1830	15.80 ⎭			
1831–1840	15.67	—	—	—
1841–1850	15.83	—	—	—
1849	15.80	5.4	7.8	1.44
1850	15.83	8.9	7.8	0.88
1851	15.46	13.5	8.0	0.59
1852	15.57	36.6	8.1	0.22
1853	15.33	31.1	8.1	0·26
1854	15.33	25.5	8.1	0.32
1855	15.36	27.0	8.1	0.30
1856	15.33	29.5	8.2	0.28
1857	15.27	26.7	8.1	0.30
1858	15.36	24.9	8.1	0.32
1859	15.21	25.0	8.2	0.33
1860	15.30	23.9	8.2	0.34
1861	15.47	22.8	8.5	0.37
1862	15.36	21.6	9.0	0.42
1863	15.38	21.4	9.8	0.46
1864	15.40	22.6	10.3	0.45
1865	15.33	24.0	10.4	0.43
1866	15.44	24.2	10.1	0.42
1867	15.57	22.8	10.8	0.48
1868	15.60	22.0	10.0	0.45
1869	15.60	21.2	9.5	0.45
1870	15.60	21.4	10.3	0.48
1871	15.59	21.4	12.2	0.57
1872	15.63	19.9	13.1	0.66
*1873	15.90	19.2	17.9	0.93
†1874	16.15	18.2	14.3	0.79
1875	16.76	19.5	16.1	0.82
1876	Highest 20.17 / Lowest 16.62 17.68	19.0	14.8	0.78
1877	Highest 17.58 / Lowest 16.84 17.22	19.4	16.2	0.84
1878	Highest 19.00 / Lowest 17.14 17.92	17.3	14.7	0.85

* Demonetisation of Silver by Germany.
† Suspension of Free Mintage of Silver by the Latin Union.

TABLE OF PRICES IN LONDON OF SILVER FROM 1827 TO 1879.

Year	Lowest	Highest	Year	Lowest	Highest	Year	Lowest	Highest
1827	$59\frac{1}{2}$	$60\frac{1}{4}$	1845	$58\frac{7}{8}$	$59\frac{7}{8}$	1863	61	$61\frac{3}{4}$
1828	$59\frac{1}{4}$	$60\frac{1}{2}$	1846	59	$60\frac{1}{8}$	1864	$60\frac{5}{8}$	$62\frac{1}{8}$
1829	$59\frac{1}{2}$	60	1847	$58\frac{7}{8}$	$60\frac{3}{8}$	1865	$60\frac{1}{8}$	$61\frac{7}{8}$
1830	$59\frac{3}{4}$	60	1848	$58\frac{1}{2}$	60	1866	$60\frac{3}{8}$	$62\frac{1}{4}$
1831	60	$60\frac{7}{8}$	1849	$59\frac{1}{2}$	$60\frac{1}{4}$	1867	$60\frac{5}{16}$	$61\frac{1}{4}$
1832	$59\frac{3}{4}$	$60\frac{1}{4}$	1850	$59\frac{1}{2}$	$61\frac{1}{2}$	1868	$60\frac{1}{8}$	$61\frac{1}{8}$
1833	$58\frac{3}{4}$	60	1851	60	$61\frac{5}{8}$	1869	60	61
1834	$59\frac{3}{4}$	$60\frac{3}{8}$	1852	$59\frac{7}{8}$	$61\frac{7}{8}$	1870	$60\frac{1}{4}$	62
1835	$59\frac{1}{4}$	60	1853	$60\frac{5}{8}$	$62\frac{3}{8}$	1871	$60\frac{3}{16}$	$60\frac{7}{8}$
1836	$59\frac{5}{8}$	$60\frac{3}{8}$	1854	$60\frac{7}{8}$	$61\frac{7}{8}$	1872	$59\frac{1}{4}$	$61\frac{3}{8}$
1837	59	$60\frac{3}{8}$	1855	60	$61\frac{5}{8}$	DEMONETISATION		
1838	$59\frac{3}{8}$	$60\frac{1}{4}$	1856	$60\frac{1}{2}$	$62\frac{1}{4}$	1873	$57\frac{7}{8}$	$59\frac{15}{16}$
1839	60	$60\frac{5}{8}$	1857	61	$62\frac{5}{8}$	1874	$57\frac{1}{4}$	$59\frac{1}{2}$
1840	$60\frac{1}{8}$	$60\frac{5}{8}$	1858	$60\frac{3}{4}$	$61\frac{7}{8}$	1875	$55\frac{1}{2}$	$57\frac{5}{8}$
1841	$59\frac{3}{4}$	$60\frac{3}{8}$	1859	$61\frac{3}{4}$	$62\frac{3}{4}$	1876	$46\frac{3}{4}$	$58\frac{1}{2}$
1842	$59\frac{1}{2}$	$59\frac{3}{4}$	1860	$61\frac{1}{4}$	$62\frac{3}{8}$	1877	$53\frac{1}{4}$	$58\frac{1}{4}$
1843	59	$59\frac{5}{8}$	1861	$60\frac{5}{8}$	$61\frac{3}{4}$	1878	$49\frac{1}{2}$	$55\frac{1}{4}$
1844	$59\frac{1}{4}$	$59\frac{3}{4}$	1862	61	$62\frac{1}{4}$	1879	49	—

This table **shows only the highest and lowest** prices, but if the total average be **taken of the mean** prices, up to 1872, before the demonetisation of silver took place, it will be found to correspond with the **Bi-metallic rate of $60\frac{7}{8}$ pence, or $15\frac{1}{2}$** of silver to 1 of gold.

H

The following figures show the result of the working of the two richest mines in America:—

Consolidated Virginia.

Year	Gold	Silver	Total
	£	£	£
1873	62,000	66,000	128,000
1874	412,000	583,000	995,000
1875	1,407,000	1,936,000	3,343,000
1876	1,475,000	1,855,000	3,330,000
1877	1,254,000	1,492,000	2,746,000
1878	754,000	845,000	1,599,000
1879	239,000	256,000	495,000
Total	£5,603,000	7,033,000	12,636,000

California.

Year	Gold	Silver	Total
	£	£	£
1876	1,298,000	1,382,000	2,680,000
1877	1,876,000	1,907,000	3,783,000
1878	1,110,000	1,079,000	2,189,000
1879	266,000	248,000	514,000
Total	4,550,000	4,616,000	9,166,000
Consolidated Virginia	5,603,000	7,033,000	12,636,000
Total	£10,153,000	11,649,000	21,802,000

The total production of America for the last ten years was as follows :—

Year	Gold	Silver
	£	£
1870	10,000,000	3,436,000
1871	9,000,000	4,952,000
1872	7,480,000	6,148,000
1873	7,480,000	7,644,000
1874	8,280,000	6,840,000
1875	8,280,000	6,840,000
1876	9,200,000	8,776,000
1877	9,360,000	8,328,000
1878	9,800,000	9,992,000
1879	8,080,000	8,728,000
1880	7,480,000	8,060,000
Total	£94,444,000	£79,744,000

On the production of 1879 the Director of the United States Mint remarks :—

'The production of 1879 is considerably less than that of the preceding year. It has resulted from the diminished yield of the mines of the Comstock Lode. A depth has been reached 1,000 feet below the bed of the Carson River, and impediments are encountered from accumulations of water and from the oppressive temperature, which discourage and have retarded vertical exploration.'

Spottiswoode & Co., Printers, New-street Square, London.

A LIST OF

KEGAN PAUL AND CO.'S

PUBLICATIONS.

12.81.

1, *Paternoster Square*, **London**.

A LIST OF
C. KEGAN PAUL AND CO.'S
PUBLICATIONS.

ADAMS (F. O.), F.R.G.S.
The History of Japan. From the Earliest Period to the Present Time. New Edition, revised. 2 volumes. With Maps and Plans. Demy 8vo. Cloth, price 21s. each.

ADAMS (W. D.).
Lyrics of Love, from Shakespeare to Tennyson. Selected and arranged by. Fcap. 8vo. Cloth extra, gilt edges, price 3s. 6d.

ADAMSON (H. T.), B.D.
The Truth as it is in Jesus. Crown 8vo. Cloth, price 8s. 6d.

The Three Sevens. Crown 8vo. Cloth, price 5s. 6d.

ADAM ST. VICTOR.
The Liturgical Poetry of Adam St. Victor. From the text of Gautier. With Translations into English in the Original Metres, and Short Explanatory Notes. By DIGBY S. WRANGHAM, M.A. 3 vols. Crown 8vo. Printed on hand-made paper. Cloth, price 21s.

A. K. H. B.
From a Quiet Place. A New Volume of Sermons. Crown 8vo. Cloth, price 5s.

ALBERT (Mary).
Holland and her Heroes to the year 1585. An Adaptation from Motley's "Rise of the Dutch Republic." Small crown 8vo. Cloth, price, 4s. 6d.

ALLEN (Rev. R.), M.A.
Abraham; his Life, Times, and Travels, 3,800 years ago. Second Edition. With Map. Post 8vo. Cloth, price 6s.

ALLEN (Grant), B.A.
Physiological Æsthetics. Large post 8vo. 9s.

ALLIES (T. W.), M.A.
Per Crucem ad Lucem. The Result of a Life. 2 vols. Demy 8vo. Cloth, price 25s.

A Life's Decision. Crown 8vo. Cloth, price 7s. 6d.

ANDERSON (Col. R. P.).
Victories and Defeats. An Attempt to explain the Causes which have led to them. An Officer's Manual. Demy 8vo. Cloth, price 14s.

ANDERSON (R. C.), C.E.
Tables for Facilitating the Calculation of every Detail in connection with Earthen and Masonry Dams. Royal 8vo. Cloth, price £2 2s.

ARCHER (Thomas).
About my Father's Business. Work amidst the Sick, the Sad, and the Sorrowing. Crown 8vo. Cloth, price 2s. 6d.

ARMSTRONG (Richard A.), B.A.
Latter-Day Teachers. Six Lectures. Small crown 8vo. Cloth, price 2s. 6d.

Army of the North German Confederation.
A Brief Description of its Organization, of the Different Branches of the Service and their rôle in War, of its Mode of Fighting, &c. &c. Translated from the Corrected Edition, by permission of the Author, by Colonel Edward Newdigate. Demy 8vo. Cloth, price 5s.

ARNOLD (Arthur).
Social Politics. Demy 8vo. Cloth, price 14s.

Free Land. Second Edition. Crown 8vo. Cloth, price 6s.

A List of C. Kegan Paul & Co.'s Publications.

AUBERTIN (J. J.).
Camoens' Lusiads. Portuguese Text, with Translation by. With Map and Portraits. 2 vols. Demy 8vo. Price 30s.

Seventy Sonnets of Camoens'. Portuguese text and translation, with some original poems. Dedicated to Captain Richard F. Burton. Printed on hand-made paper. Cloth, bevelled boards, gilt top, price 7s. 6d.

Aunt Mary's Bran Pie.
By the author of "St. Olave's." Illustrated. Cloth, price 3s. 6d.

AVIA.
The Odyssey of Homer Done into English Verse. Fcap. 4to. Cloth, price 15s.

BADGER (George Perry), D.C.L.
An English-Arabic Lexicon. In which the equivalents for English words and idiomatic sentences are rendered into literary and colloquial Arabic. Royal 4to. Cloth, price £9 9s.

BAGEHOT (Walter).
Some Articles on the Depreciation of Silver, and Topics connected with it. Demy 8vo. Price 5s.

The English Constitution. A New Edition, Revised and Corrected, with an Introductory Dissertation on Recent Changes and Events. Crown 8vo. Cloth, price 7s. 6d.

Lombard Street. A Description of the Money Market. Seventh Edition. Crown 8vo. Cloth, price 7s. 6d.

BAGOT (Alan).
Accidents in Mines: their Causes and Prevention. Crown 8vo. Cloth, price 6s.

BAKER (Sir Sherston, Bart.).
Halleck's International Law; or Rules Regulating the Intercourse of States in Peace and War. A New Edition, Revised, with Notes and Cases. 2 vols. Demy 8vo. Cloth, price 38s.

BAKER (Sir Sherston, Bart.)—
continued.
The Laws relating to Quarantine. Crown 8vo. Cloth, price 12s. 6d.

BALDWIN (Capt. J. H.), F.Z.S.
The Large and Small Game of Bengal and the North-Western Provinces of India. 4to. With numerous Illustrations. Second Edition. Cloth, price 21s.

BALLIN (Ada S. and F. L.).
A Hebrew Grammar. With Exercises selected from the Bible. Crown 8vo. Cloth, price 7s. 6d.

BANKS (Mrs. G. L.).
God's Providence House. New Edition. Crown 8vo. Cloth, price 3s. 6d.

Ripples and Breakers. Poems. Square 8vo. Cloth, price 5s.

BARCLAY (Edgar).
Mountain Life in Algeria. Crown 4to. With numerous Illustrations by Photogravure. Cloth, price 16s.

BARLEE (Ellen).
Locked Out: a Tale of the Strike. With a Frontispiece. Royal 16mo. Cloth, price 1s. 6d.

BARNES (William).
An Outline of English Speechcraft. Crown 8vo. Cloth, price 4s.

Poems of Rural Life, in the Dorset Dialect. New Edition, complete in 1 vol. Crown 8vo. Cloth, price 8s. 6d.

Outlines of Redecraft (Logic). With English Wording. Crown 8vo. Cloth, price 3s.

BARTLEY (George C. T.).
Domestic Economy: Thrift in Every Day Life. Taught in Dialogues suitable for Children of all ages. Small crown 8vo. Cloth, limp, 2s.

BAUR (Ferdinand), Dr. **Ph.**
A Philological Introduction to Greek and Latin for Students. Translated and adapted from the German of. By C. KEGAN PAUL, M.A. Oxon., and the Rev. E. D. STONE, M.A., late Fellow of King's College, Cambridge, and Assistant Master at Eton. Second and revised edition. Crown 8vo. Cloth, price 6s.

BAYNES (Rev. Canon R. H.).
At the Communion Time. A Manual for Holy Communion. With a preface by the Right Rev. the Lord Bishop of Derry and Raphoe. Cloth, price 1s. 6d.
*** Can also be had bound in French morocco, price 2s. 6d.; Persian morocco, price 3s.; Calf, or Turkey morocco, price 3s. 6d.

Home Songs for Quiet Hours. Fourth and Cheaper Edition. Fcap. 8vo. Cloth, price 2s. 6d.
This may also be had handsomely bound in morocco with gilt edges.

BELLINGHAM (Henry), Barrister-at-Law.
Social Aspects of Catholicism and Protestantism in their Civil Bearing upon Nations. Translated and adapted from the French of M. le Baron de Haulleville. With a Preface by His Eminence Cardinal Manning. Second and cheaper edition. Crown 8vo. Cloth, price 3s. 6d.

BENNETT (Dr. W. C.).
Narrative Poems & Ballads. Fcap. 8vo. Sewed in Coloured Wrapper, price 1s.

Songs for Sailors. Dedicated by Special Request to H. R. H. the Duke of Edinburgh. With Steel Portrait and Illustrations. Crown 8vo. Cloth, price 3s. 6d.
An Edition in Illustrated Paper Covers, price 1s.

Songs of a Song Writer. Crown 8vo. Cloth, price 6s.

BENT (J. Theodore).
Genoa. How the Republic Rose and Fell. With 18 Illustrations. Demy 8vo. Cloth, price 18s.

BETHAM - EDWARDS (Miss M.).
Kitty. With a Frontispiece. Crown 8vo. Cloth, price 6s.

BEVINGTON **(L. S.).**
Key Notes. Small crown 8vo. Cloth, price 5s.

Blue Roses; or, Helen Malinofska's Marriage. By the Author of "Véra." 2 vols. Fifth Edition. Cloth, gilt tops, 12s.
*** Also a Cheaper Edition in 1 vol. With Frontispiece. Crown **8vo.** Cloth, price 6s.

BLUME (Major W.).
The Operations of the German Armies in France, from Sedan to the end of the war of 1870-71. With Map. From the Journals of the Head-quarters Staff. Translated by the late E. M. Jones, Maj. 20th Foot, Prof. of Mil. Hist., Sandhurst. Demy 8vo. Cloth, price 9s.

BOGUSLAWSKI (Capt. A. von).
Tactical Deductions from the War of 1870-71. Translated by Colonel Sir Lumley Graham, Bart., late 18th (Royal Irish) Regiment. Third Edition, Revised and Corrected. Demy 8vo. Cloth, price 7s.

BONWICK (J.), F.R.G.S.
Egyptian Belief and Modern Thought. Large post 8vo. Cloth, price 10s. 6d.
Pyramid Facts and Fancies. Crown 8vo. Cloth, price 5s.
The Tasmanian Lily. With Frontispiece. Crown 8vo. Cloth, price 5s.
Mike Howe, the Bushranger of Van Diemen's Land. With Frontispiece. New and cheaper edition. Crown 8vo. Cloth, price 3s. 6d.

BOWEN (H. C.), M. A.
English Grammar for Beginners. Fcap. 8vo. Cloth, price 1s.
Studies in English, for the use of Modern Schools. Small crown 8vo. Cloth, price 1s. 6d.
Simple English Poems. English Literature for Junior Classes. In Four Parts. Parts I. and II., price 6d. each, now ready.

BOWRING (Sir John).
Autobiographical Recollections. With Memoir by Lewin B. Bowring. Demy 8vo. Price 14s.

Brave Men's Footsteps.
By the Editor of "Men who have Risen." A Book of Example and Anecdote for Young People. With Four Illustrations by C. Doyle. Sixth Edition. Crown 8vo. Cloth, price 3s. 6d.

BRIALMONT (Col. A.).
Hasty Intrenchments. Translated by Lieut. Charles A. Empson, R.A. With Nine Plates. Demy 8vo. Cloth, price 6s.

BRIDGETT (Rev. J. E.).
History of the Holy Eucharist in Great Britain. 2 vols., demy 8vo. Cloth, price 18s.

BRODRICK (The Hon. G. C.).
Political Studies. Demy 8vo. Cloth, price 14s.

BROOKE (Rev. S. A.), M.A.
The Late Rev. F. W. Robertson, M.A., Life and Letters of. Edited by.
  I. Uniform with the Sermons. 2 vols. With Steel Portrait. Price 7s. 6d.
  II. Library Edition. 8vo. With Portrait. Price 12s.
  III. A Popular Edition, in 1 vol. 8vo. Price 6s.

Sermons. First Series. Twelfth and Cheaper Edition. Crown 8vo. Cloth, price 5s.

Sermons. Second Series. Fifth and Cheaper Edition. Crown 8vo. Cloth, price 5s.

Theology in the English Poets. — COWPER, COLERIDGE, WORDSWORTH, and BURNS. Fourth and Cheaper Edition. Post 8vo. Cloth, price 5s.

Christ in Modern Life. Fifteenth and Cheaper Edition. Crown 8vo. Cloth, price 5s.

The Spirit of the Christian Life. A New Volume of Sermons. Second Edition. Crown 8vo. Cloth, price 7s. 6d.

The Fight of Faith. Sermons preached on various occasions. Fifth Edition. Crown 8vo. Cloth, price 7s. 6d.

BROOKE (W. G.), M.A.
The Public Worship Regulation Act. With a Classified Statement of its Provisions, Notes, and Index. Third Edition, Revised and Corrected. Crown 8vo. Cloth, price 2s. 6d.

Six Privy Council Judgments—1850-1872. Annotated by. Third Edition. Crown 8vo. Cloth, price 9s.

BROUN (J. A.).
Magnetic Observations at Trevandrum and Augustia Malley. Vol. I. 4to. Cloth, price 63s.

The Report from above, separately sewed, price 21s.

BROWN (Rev. J. Baldwin).
The Higher Life. Its Reality, Experience, and Destiny. Fifth and Cheaper Edition. Crown 8vo. Cloth, price 5s.

Doctrine of Annihilation in the Light of the Gospel of Love. Five Discourses. Third Edition. Crown 8vo. Cloth, price 2s. 6d.

The Christian Policy of Life. A Book for Young Men of Business. New and Cheaper Edition. Crown 8vo. Cloth, price 3s. 6d.

BROWN (J. Croumbie), LL.D.
Reboisement in France; or, Records of the Replanting of the Alps, the Cevennes, and the Pyrenees with Trees, Herbage, and Bush. Demy 8vo. Cloth, price 12s. 6d.

The Hydrology of Southern Africa. Demy 8vo. Cloth, price 10s. 6d.

BROWNE (W. R.).
The Inspiration of the New Testament. With a Preface by the Rev. J. P. NORRIS, D.D. Fcap. 8vo. Cloth, price 2s. 6d.

BRYANT (W. C.)
Poems. Red-line Edition. With 24 Illustrations and Portrait of the Author. Crown 8vo. Cloth extra, price 7s. 6d.

A Cheaper Edition, with Frontispiece. Small crown 8vo. Cloth, price 3s. 6d.

BURCKHARDT (Jacob).
The Civilization of the Period of the Renaissance in Italy. Authorized translation, by S. G. C. Middlemore. 2 vols. Demy 8vo. Cloth, price 24s.

BURTON (Mrs. Richard).
The Inner Life of Syria, Palestine, and the Holy Land. With Maps, Photographs, and Coloured Plates. 2 vols. Second Edition. Demy 8vo. Cloth, price 24s.

*** Also a Cheaper Edition in one volume. Large post 8vo. Cloth, price 10s. 6d.

BURTON (Capt. Richard F.).
The Gold Mines of Midian and the Ruined Midianite Cities. A Fortnight's Tour in North Western Arabia. With numerous Illustrations. Second Edition. Demy 8vo. Cloth, price 18s.

The Land of Midian Revisited. With numerous illustrations on wood and by Chromolithography. 2 vols. Demy 8vo. Cloth, price 32s.

BUSBECQ (Ogier Ghiselin de).
His Life and Letters. By Charles Thornton Forster, M.D. and F. H. Blackburne Daniell, M.D. 2 vols. With Frontispieces. Demy 8vo. Cloth, price 24s.

BUTLER (Alfred J.).
Amaranth and Asphodel. Songs from the Greek Anthology.—I. Songs of the Love of Women. II. Songs of the Love of Nature. III. Songs of Death. IV. Songs of Hereafter. Small crown 8vo. Cloth, price 2s.

CALDERON.
Calderon's Dramas: The Wonder-Working Magician—Life is a Dream—The Purgatory of St. Patrick. Translated by Denis Florence MacCarthy. Post 8vo. Cloth, price 10s.

CANDLER (H.).
The Groundwork of Belief. Crown 8vo. Cloth, price 7s.

CARPENTER (W. B.), M.D.
The Principles of Mental Physiology. With their Applications to the Training and Discipline of the Mind, and the Study of its Morbid Conditions. Illustrated. Fifth Edition. 8vo. Cloth, price 12s.

CARPENTER (Dr. Philip P.).
His Life and Work. Edited by his brother, Russell Lant Carpenter. With portrait and vignette. Second Edition. Crown 8vo. Cloth, price 7s. 6d.

CAVALRY OFFICER.
Notes on Cavalry Tactics, Organization, &c. With Diagrams Demy 8vo. Cloth, price 12s.

CERVANTES.
The Ingenious Knight Don Quixote de la Mancha. A New Translation from the Originals of 1605 and 1608. By A. J. Duffield With Notes. 3 vols. demy 8vo. Cloth, price 42s.

CHAPMAN (Hon. Mrs. E. W.).
A Constant Heart. A Story. 2 vols. Cloth, gilt tops, price 12s.

CHEYNE (Rev. T. K.).
The Prophecies of Isaiah. Translated, with Critical Notes and Dissertations by. Two vols., demy 8vo. Cloth, price 25s.

Children's Toys, and some Elementary Lessons in General Knowledge which they teach. Illustrated. Crown 8vo. Cloth, price 5s.

Clairaut's Elements of Geometry. Translated by Dr. Kaines, with 145 figures. Crown 8vo. Cloth, price 4s. 6d.

CLARKE (Mary Cowden).
Honey from the Weed. Crown 8vo. Cloth, price 7s.

CLAYDEN (P. W.).
England under Lord Beaconsfield. The Political History of the Last Six Years, from the end of 1873 to the beginning of 1880. Second Edition. With Index, and Continuation to March, 1880. Demy 8vo. Cloth, price 16s.

CLERY (C.), Lieut.-Col.
Minor Tactics. With 26 Maps and Plans. Fifth and Revised Edition. Demy 8vo. Cloth, price 16s.

CLODD (Edward), F.R.A.S.
The Childhood of the World: a Simple Account of Man in Early Times. Sixth Edition. Crown 8vo. Cloth, price 3s.
A Special Edition for Schools. Price 1s.

The Childhood of Religions. Including a Simple Account of the Birth and Growth of Myths and Legends. Third Thousand. Crown 8vo. Cloth, price 5s.
A Special Edition for Schools. Price 1s. 6d.

Jesus of Nazareth. With a brief Sketch of Jewish History to the Time of His Birth. Small crown 8vo. Cloth, price 6s.

COGHLAN (J. Cole), D.D.
The Modern Pharisee and other Sermons. Edited by the Very Rev. A. H. Dickinson, D.D., Dean of Chapel Royal, Dublin. New and cheaper edition. Crown 8vo. Cloth, price 7s. 6d.

COLERIDGE (Sara).
Pretty Lessons in Verse for Good Children, with some Lessons in Latin, in Easy Rhyme. A New Edition. Illustrated. Fcap. 8vo. Cloth, price 3s. 6d.

Phantasmion. A Fairy Tale. With an Introductory Preface by the Right Hon. Lord Coleridge, of Ottery St. Mary. A New Edition. Illustrated. Crown 8vo. Cloth, price 7s. 6d.

Memoir and Letters of Sara Coleridge. Edited by her Daughter. Cheap Edition. With one Portrait. Cloth, price 7s. 6d.

COLLINS (Mortimer).
The Secret of Long Life. Small crown 8vo. Cloth, price 3s. 6d.
Inn of Strange Meetings, and other Poems. Crown 8vo. Cloth, price 5s.

CONNELL (A. K.).
Discontent and Danger in India. Small crown 8vo. Cloth, price 3s. 6d.

COOKE (Prof. J. P.)
Scientific Culture. Crown 8vo. Cloth, price 1s.

COOPER (H. J.).
The Art of Furnishing on Rational and Æsthetic Principles. New and Cheaper Edition. Fcap. 8vo. Cloth, price 1s. 6d.

COPPÉE (François).
L'Exilée. Done into English Verse with the sanction of the Author by I. O. L. Crown 8vo. Vellum, price 5s.

CORFIELD (Prof.), M.D.
Health. Crown 8vo. Cloth, price 6s.

CORY (Col. Arthur).
The Eastern Menace. Crown 8vo. Cloth, price 7s. 6d.

CORY (William).
A Guide to Modern English History. Part I. MDCCCXV.—MDCCCXXX. Demy 8vo. Cloth, price 9s.

COURTNEY (W. L.).
The Metaphysics of John Stuart Mill. Crown 8vo. Cloth, price 5s. 6d.

COX (Rev. Sir G. W.), Bart.
A History of Greece from the Earliest Period to the end of the Persian War. New Edition. 2 vols. Demy 8vo. Cloth, price 36s.

A General History of Greece from the Earliest Period to the Death of Alexander the Great, with a sketch of the subsequent History to the present time. New Edition. Crown 8vo. Cloth, price 7s. 6d.

Tales of Ancient Greece. New Edition. Small crown 8vo. Cloth, price 6s.

School History of Greece. With Maps. New Edition. Fcap. 8vo. Cloth, price 3s. 6d.

The Great Persian War from the Histories of Herodotus. New Edition. Fcap. 8vo. Cloth, price 3s. 6d.

A Manual of Mythology in the form of Question and Answer. New Edition. Fcap. 8vo. Cloth, price 3s.

COX (Rev. Sir G. W.), Bart.—
  continued.
  An Introduction to the Science of Comparative Mythology and Folk-Lore. Large crown 8vo. Cloth, price 9s.

COX (Rev. Sir G. W.), Bart., M.A., and EUSTACE HINTON JONES.
  Popular Romances of the Middle Ages. Second Edition in one volume. Crown 8vo. Cloth, price 6s.

COX (Rev. Samuel).
  A Commentary on the Book of Job. With a Translation. Demy 8vo. Cloth, price 15s.
  Salvator Mundi; or, Is Christ the Saviour of all Men? Sixth Edition. Crown 8vo. Cloth, price 5s.
  The Genesis of Evil, and other Sermons, mainly Expository. Second Edition. Crown 8vo. Cloth, price 6s.

CRAUFURD (A. H.).
  Seeking for Light: Sermons. Crown 8vo. Cloth, price 5s.

CRAVEN (Mrs.).
  A Year's Meditations. Crown 8vo. Cloth, price 6s.

CRAWFURD (Oswald).
  Portugal, Old and New. With Illustrations and Maps. New and Cheaper Edition. Crown 8vo. Cloth, price 6s.

CRESSWELL (Mrs. G.).
  The King's Banner. Drama in Four Acts. Five Illustrations. 4to. Cloth, price 10s. 6d.

CROZIER (John Beattie), M.B.
  The Religion of the Future. Crown 8vo. Cloth, price 6s.

Cyclopædia of Common Things. Edited by the Rev. Sir George W. Cox, Bart., M.A. With 500 Illustrations. Large post 8vo. Cloth, price 7s. 6d.

DALTON (John Neale), M.A., R.N.
  Sermons to Naval Cadets. Preached on board H.M.S. "Britannia." Second Edition. Small crown 8vo. Cloth, price 3s. 6d.

D'ANVERS (N. R.).
  Parted. A Tale of Clouds and Sunshine. With 4 Illustrations. Extra Fcap. 8vo. Cloth, price 3s. 6d.
  Little Minnie's Troubles. An Every-day Chronicle. With Four Illustrations by W. H. Hughes. Fcap. Cloth, price 3s. 6d.
  Pixie's Adventures; or, the Tale of a Terrier. With 21 Illustrations. 16mo. Cloth, price 4s. 6d.
  Nanny's Adventures; or, the Tale of a Goat. With 12 Illustrations. 16mo. Cloth, price 4s. 6d.

DAVIDSON (Rev. Samuel), D.D., LL.D.
  The New Testament, translated from the Latest Greek Text of Tischendorf. A New and thoroughly Revised Edition. Post 8vo. Cloth, price 10s. 6d.
  Canon of the Bible: Its Formation, History, and Fluctuations. Third Edition, revised and enlarged. Small crown 8vo. Cloth, price 5s.

DAVIES (G. Christopher).
  Rambles and Adventures of Our School Field Club. With Four Illustrations. New and Cheaper Edition. Crown 8vo. Cloth, price 3s. 6d.

DAVIES (Rev. J. L.), M.A.
  Theology and Morality. Essays on Questions of Belief and Practice. Crown 8vo. Cloth, price 7s. 6d.

DAVIES (T. Hart.).
  Catullus. Translated into English Verse. Crown 8vo. Cloth, price 6s.

DAWSON (George), M.A.
  The Authentic Gospel. A New Volume of Sermons. Edited by George St. Clair. Crown 8vo. Cloth, price 6s.
  Prayers, with a Discourse on Prayer. Edited by his Wife. Sixth Edition. Crown 8vo. Price 6s.

DAWSON (George), M.A.—*continued.*
  Sermons on Disputed Points and Special Occasions. Edited by his Wife. Third Edition. Crown 8vo. Cloth, price 6s.

  Sermons on Daily Life and Duty. Edited by his Wife. Third Edition. Crown 8vo. Cloth, price 6s.

DE L'HOSTE (Col. E. P.).
  The Desert Pastor, Jean Jarousseau. Translated from the French of Eugène Pelletan. With a Frontispiece. New Edition. Fcap. 8vo. Cloth, price 3s. 6d.

DE REDCLIFFE (Viscount Stratford), P.C., K.G., G.C.B.
  Why am I a Christian? Fifth Edition. Crown 8vo. Cloth, price 3s.

DESPREZ (Philip S.).
  Daniel and John; or, the Apocalypse of the Old and that of the New Testament. Demy 8vo. Cloth, price 12s.

DE TOCQUEVILLE (A.).
  Correspondence and Conversations of, with Nassau William Senior, from 1834 to 1859. Edited by M. C. M. Simpson. 2 vols. Post 8vo. Cloth, price 21s.

DE VERE (Aubrey).
  Legends of the Saxon Saints. Small crown 8vo. Cloth, price 6s.

  Alexander the Great. A Dramatic Poem. Small crown 8vo. Cloth, price 5s.

  The Infant Bridal, and other Poems. A New and Enlarged Edition. Fcap. 8vo. Cloth, price 7s. 6d.

  The Legends of St. Patrick, and other Poems. Small crown 8vo. Cloth, price 5s.

  St. Thomas of Canterbury. A Dramatic Poem. Large fcap. 8vo. Cloth, price 5s.

  Antar and Zara: an Eastern Romance. INISFAIL, and other Poems, Meditative and Lyrical. Fcap. 8vo. Price 6s.

DE VERE (Aubrey)—*continued.*
  The Fall of Rora, the Search after Proserpine, and other Poems, Meditative and Lyrical. Fcap. 8vo. Price 6s.

DOBELL (Mrs. Horace).
  Ethelstone, Eveline, and other Poems. Crown 8vo. Cloth, price 6s.

DOBSON (Austin).
  Vignettes in Rhyme and Vers de Société. Third Edition. Fcap. 8vo. Cloth, price 5s.

  Proverbs in Porcelain. By the Author of "Vignettes in Rhyme." Second Edition. Crown 8vo. 6s.

  Dorothy. A Country Story in Elegiac Verse. With Preface. Demy 8vo. Cloth, price 5s.

DOWDEN (Edward), LL.D.
  Shakspere: a Critical Study of his Mind and Art. Fifth Edition. Large post 8vo. Cloth, price 12s.

  Studies in Literature, 1789-1877. Large post 8vo. Cloth, price 12s.

  Poems. Second Edition. Fcap. 8vo. Cloth, price 5s.

DOWNTON (Rev. H.), M.A.
  Hymns and Verses. Original and Translated. Small crown 8vo. Cloth, price 3s. 6d.

DREWRY (G. O.), M.D.
  The Common-Sense Management of the Stomach. Fifth Edition. Fcap. 8vo. Cloth, price 2s. 6d.

DREWRY (G. O.), M.D., and BARTLETT (H. C.), Ph.D., F.C.S.
  Cup and Platter: or, Notes on Food and its Effects. New and cheaper Edition. Small 8vo. Cloth, price 1s. 6d.

DRUMMOND (Miss).
  Tripps Buildings. A Study from Life, with Frontispiece. Small crown 8vo. Cloth, price 3s. 6d.

A 2

DUFFIELD (A. J.).
Don Quixote. His Critics and Commentators. With a Brief Account of the Minor Works of Miguel de Cervantes Saavedra, and a statement of the end and aim of the greatest of them all. A Handy Book for General Readers. Crown 8vo. Cloth, price 3s. 6d.

DU MONCEL (Count).
The Telephone, the Microphone, and the Phonograph. With 74 Illustrations. Small crown 8vo. Cloth, price 5s.

DUTT (Toru).
A Sheaf Gleaned in French Fields. New Edition, with Portrait. Demy 8vo. Cloth, price 10s. 6d.

DU VERNOIS (Col. von Verdy).
Studies in leading Troops. An authorized and accurate Translation by Lieutenant H. J. T. Hildyard, 71st Foot. Parts I. and II. Demy 8vo. Cloth, price 7s.

EDEN (Frederick).
The Nile without a Dragoman. Second Edition. Crown 8vo. Cloth, price 7s. 6d.

EDGEWORTH (F. Y.).
Mathematical Psychics: an Essay on the Application of Mathematics to Social Science. Demy 8vo. Cloth, price 7s. 6d.

EDIS (Robert W.).
Decoration and Furniture of Town Houses. A series of Cantor Lectures delivered before the Society of Arts, 1880. Amplified and enlarged, with 29 full-page Illustrations and numerous sketches. Second Edition. Square 8vo. Cloth, price 12s. 6d.

EDMONDS (Herbert).
Well Spent Lives: a Series of Modern Biographies. New and Cheaper Edition. Crown 8vo. Price 3s. 6d.

Educational Code of the Prussian Nation, in its Present **Form**. In accordance with the Decisions of the Common Provincial Law, and with those of Recent Legislation. Crown 8vo. Cloth, price 2s. 6d.

THE EDUCATION LIBRARY (Edited by Philip Magnus).
An Introduction to the History of Educational Theories. By OSCAR BROWNING, M.A. Cloth, price 3s. 6d.
John Amos Comenius: his Life and Educational Work. By Prof. S. S. LAURIE, A.M. Cloth, price 3s. 6d.
Old Greek **Education**. By the Rev. Prof. MAHAFFY, M.A. Cloth, price 3s. 6d.

EDWARDS (Rev. Basil).
Minor Chords; or, Songs for the Suffering: a Volume of Verse. Fcap. 8vo. Cloth, price 3s. 6d.; paper, price 2s. 6d.

ELLIOT (Lady Charlotte).
Medusa and other Poems. Crown 8vo. Cloth, price 6s.

ELLIOTT (Ebenezer), The Corn Law Rhymer.
Poems. Edited by his Son, the Rev. Edwin Elliott, of St. John's, Antigua. 2 vols. Crown 8vo. Cloth, price 18s.

ELSDALE (Henry).
Studies in Tennyson's Idylls. Crown 8vo. Cloth, price 5s.

ELYOT (Sir Thomas).
The Boke named the Gouernour. Edited from the First Edition of 1531 by Henry Herbert Stephen Croft, M.A., Barrister-at-Law. With Portraits of Sir Thomas and Lady Elyot, copied by permission of her Majesty from Holbein's Original Drawings at Windsor Castle. 2 vols. fcap. 4to. Cloth, price 50s.

Epic of Hades (The).
By the author of "Songs of Two Worlds." Twelfth Edition. Fcap. 8vo. Cloth, price 7s. 6d.
*** Also an Illustrated Edition with seventeen full-page designs in photomezzotint by GEORGE R. CHAPMAN. 4to. Cloth, extra gilt leaves, price 25s. and a Large Paper Edition, with portrait, price 10s. 6d.

EVANS (Anne).
Poems and Music. With Memorial Preface by Ann Thackeray Ritchie. Large crown 8vo. Cloth, price 7s. 6d.

EVANS (Mark).
The Gospel of Home Life.
Crown 8vo. Cloth, price 4s. 6d.

The Story of our Father's
Love, told to Children. Fourth
and Cheaper Edition. With Four
Illustrations. Fcap. 8vo. Cloth,
price 1s. 6d.

A Book of Common Prayer
and Worship for Household
Use, compiled exclusively from the
Holy Scriptures. New and Cheaper
Edition. Fcap. 8vo. Cloth, price 1s.

The King's **Story Book.**
In three parts. Fcap. 8vo. Cloth,
price 1s. 6d. each.
*** Parts I. and II., with eight illustrations and two Picture Maps, now ready.

EX-CIVILIAN.
Life in the Mofussil; or,
Civilian Life in Lower Bengal. 2
vols. Large post 8vo. Price 14s.

FARQUHARSON (M.).
I. Elsie Dinsmore. Crown
8vo. Cloth, price 3s. 6d.
II. Elsie's Girlhood. Crown
8vo. Cloth, price 3s. 6d.
III. Elsie's Holidays at
Roselands. Crown 8vo.
Cloth, price 3s. 6d.

FELKIN (H. M.).
Technical Education in a
Saxon Town. Published for the
City and Guilds of London Institute
for the Advancement of Technical
Education. Demy 8vo. Cloth, price
2s.

FIELD (Horace), B.A. Lond.
The Ultimate Triumph of
Christianity. Small crown 8vo.
Cloth, price 3s. 6d.

FINN (the late James), M.R.A.S.
Stirring Times; or, Records
from Jerusalem Consular Chronicles
of 1853 to 1856. Edited and Compiled by his Widow. With a Preface
by the Viscountess STRANGFORD.
2 vols. Demy 8vo. Price 30s.

FLOREDICE (W. H.).
A Month among the Mere
Irish. Small crown 8vo. Cloth,
price 5s.

Folkestone Ritual Case
(The). The Argument, Proceedings,
Judgment, and Report, revised by
the several Counsel engaged. Demy
8vo. Cloth, price 25s.

FORMBY (Rev. Henry).
Ancient Rome and its Connection with the Christian Religion: an Outline of the History of
the City from its First Foundation
down to the Erection of the Chair
of St. Peter, A.D. 42-47. With
numerous Illustrations of Ancient
Monuments, Sculpture, and Coinage,
and of the Antiquities of the Christian Catacombs. Royal 4to. Cloth
extra, price 50s. Roxburgh, half-morocco, price 52s. 6d.

FOWLE (Rev. T. W.), M.A.
The Reconciliation of Religion and Science. Being Essays
on Immortality, Inspiration, Miracles, and the Being of Christ. Demy
8vo. Cloth, price 10s. 6d.

The Divine Legation of
Christ. Crown 8vo. Cloth, price 7s.

FRASER (Donald).
Exchange Tables of Sterling and Indian Rupee Currency, upon a new and extended system, embracing Values from One
Farthing to One Hundred Thousand
Pounds, and at Rates progressing, in
Sixteenths of a Penny, from 1s. 9d. to
2s. 3d. per Rupee. Royal 8vo.
Cloth, price 10s. 6d.

FRISWELL (J. Hain).
The Better Self. Essays for
Home Life. Crown 8vo. Cloth,
price 6s.

One of Two; or, A Left-Handed Bride. With a Frontispiece. Crown 8vo. Cloth, price 3s. 6d.

GARDINER (Samuel R.) and J.
BASS MULLINGER, M.A.
Introduction to the Study
of English History. Large crown
8vo. Cloth, price 9s.

GARDNER (J.), M.D.
Longevity: The Means of
Prolonging Life after Middle
Age. Fourth Edition, Revised and
Enlarged. Small crown 8vo. Cloth,
price 4s.

GARRETT (E.).
  By Still Waters. A Story for Quiet Hours. With Seven Illustrations. Crown 8vo. Cloth, price 6s.

GEBLER (Karl Von).
  Galileo Galilei and the Roman Curia, from Authentic Sources. Translated with the sanction of the Author, by Mrs. GEORGE STURGE. Demy 8vo. Cloth, price 12s.

GEDDES (James).
  History of the Administration of John de Witt, Grand Pensionary of Holland. Vol. I. 1623–1654. Demy 8vo., with Portrait. Cloth, price 15s.

GENNA (E.).
  Irresponsible Philanthropists. Being some Chapters on the Employment of Gentlewomen. Small crown 8vo. Cloth, price 2s. 6d.

GEORGE (Henry).
  Progress and Poverty. An Inquiry into the Cause of Industrial Depressions and of Increase of Want with Increase of Wealth. The Remedy. Post 8vo. Cloth, price 7s. 6d.

GILBERT (Mrs.).
  Autobiography and other Memorials. Edited by Josiah Gilbert. Third Edition. With Portrait and several Wood Engravings. Crown 8vo. Cloth, price 7s. 6d.

GLOVER (F.), M.A.
  Exempla Latina. A First Construing Book with Short Notes, Lexicon, and an Introduction to the Analysis of Sentences. Fcap. 8vo. Cloth, price 2s.

GODWIN (William).
  William Godwin: His Friends and Contemporaries. With Portraits and Facsimiles of the handwriting of Godwin and his Wife. By C. Kegan Paul. 2 vols. Demy 8vo. Cloth, price 28s.

  The Genius of Christianity Unveiled. Being Essays never before published. Edited, with a Preface, by C. Kegan Paul. Crown 8vo. Cloth, price 7s. 6d.

GOETZE (Capt. A. von).
  Operations of the German Engineers during the War of 1870-1871. Published by Authority, and in accordance with Official Documents. Translated from the German by Colonel G. Graham, V.C., C.B., R.E. With 6 large Maps. Demy 8vo. Cloth, **price 21s.**

GOLDSMID (Sir Francis Henry).
  Memoir of. With Portrait. Crown 8vo. Cloth, price 5s.

GOODENOUGH (Commodore J. G.), R.N., C.B., C.M.G.
  Memoir of, with Extracts from his Letters and Journals. Edited by his Widow. With Steel Engraved Portrait. Square 8vo. Cloth, 5s.
  *** Also a Library Edition with Maps, Woodcuts, and Steel Engraved Portrait. Square post 8vo. Cloth, price 14s.

GOSSE (Edmund W.).
  Studies in the Literature of Northern Europe. With a Frontispiece designed and etched by Alma Tadema. Large post 8vo. Cloth, price 12s.

  New Poems. Crown 8vo. Cloth, price 7s. **6d.**

GOULD (Rev. S. Baring), M.A.
  Germany, Present and Past. New and Cheaper Edition. Large crown 8vo. Cloth, price 7s. 6d.

  The Vicar of Morwenstow: a Memoir of the Rev. R. S. Hawker. With Portrait. Third Edition, revised. Square post 8vo. Cloth, 10s. 6d.

GRAHAM (William), M.A.
  The Creed of Science: Religious, Moral, and Social. Demy 8vo. Cloth, price 12s.

GRIFFITH (Thomas), A.M.
  The Gospel of the Divine Life. A Study of the Fourth Evangelist. Demy 8vo. Cloth, price 14s.

GRIMLEY (Rev. H. N.), M.A.
  Tremadoc Sermons, chiefly on the SPIRITUAL BODY, the UNSEEN WORLD, and the DIVINE HUMANITY. Second Edition. Crown 8vo. Cloth, price 6s.

GRÜNER (M. L.).
Studies of Blast Furnace Phenomena. Translated by L. D. B. Gordon, F.R.S.E., F.G.S. Demy 8vo. Cloth, price 7s. 6d.

GURNEY (Rev. Archer).
Words of Faith and Cheer. A Mission of Instruction and Suggestion. Crown 8vo. Cloth, price 6s.

Gwen: A Drama in Monologue. By the Author of the "Epic of Hades." Third Edition. Fcap. 8vo. Cloth, price 5s.

HAECKEL (Prof. Ernst).
The History of Creation. Translation revised by Professor E. Ray Lankester, M.A., F.R.S. With Coloured Plates and Genealogical Trees of the various groups of both plants and animals. 2 vols. Second Edition. Post 8vo. Cloth, price 32s.

The History of the Evolution of Man. With numerous Illustrations. 2 vols. Large post 8vo. Cloth, price 32s.

Freedom in Science and Teaching. From the German of Ernst Haeckel, with a Prefatory Note by T. H. Huxley, F.R.S. Crown 8vo. Cloth, price 5s.

HALF-CROWN SERIES.
Sister Dora: a Biography. By Margaret Lonsdale.
True Words for Brave Men. A Book for Soldiers and Sailors. By the late Charles Kingsley.
An Inland Voyage. By R. L. Stevenson.
Travels with a Donkey. By R. L. Stevenson.
A Nook in the Apennines. By Leader Scott.
Notes of Travel. Being Extracts from the Journals of Count Von Moltke.
Letters from Russia. By Count Von Moltke.
English Sonnets. Collected and Arranged by J. Dennis.
Lyrics of Love from Shakespeare to Tennyson. Selected and Arranged by W. D. Adams.
London Lyrics. By Frederick Locker.

HALF-CROWN SERIES—continued.
Home Songs for Quiet Hours. By the Rev. Canon R. H. Baynes.

Halleck's International Law; or, Rules Regulating the Intercourse of States in Peace and War. A New Edition, revised, with Notes and Cases. By Sir Sherston Baker, Bart. 2 vols. Demy 8vo. Cloth, price 38s.

HARDY (Thomas).
A Pair of Blue Eyes. New Edition. With Frontispiece. Crown 8vo. Cloth, price 6s.
The Return of the Native. New Edition. With Frontispiece. Crown 8vo. Cloth, price 6s.

HARRISON (Lieut.-Col. R.).
The Officer's Memorandum Book for Peace and War. Third Edition. Oblong 32mo. roan, with pencil, price 3s. 6d.

HARTINGTON (The Right Hon. the Marquis of), M.P.
Election Speeches in 1879 and 1880. With Address to the Electors of North-East Lancashire. Crown 8vo. Cloth, price 3s. 6d.

HAWEIS (Rev. H. R.), M.A.
Arrows in the Air. Crown 8vo. Fourth and Cheaper Edition. Cloth, price 5s.
Current Coin. Materialism—The Devil—Crime—Drunkenness—Pauperism—Emotion—Recreation—The Sabbath. Fourth and Cheaper Edition. Crown 8vo. Cloth, price 5s.
Speech in Season. Fifth and Cheaper Edition. Crown 8vo. Cloth, price 5s.
Thoughts for the Times. Twelfth and Cheaper Edition. Crown 8vo. Cloth, price 5s.
Unsectarian Family Prayers. New and Cheaper Edition. Fcap. 8vo. Cloth, price 1s. 6d.

HAWKER (Robert Stephen).
The Poetical Works of. Now first collected and arranged with a prefatory notice by J. G. Godwin. With Portrait. Crown 8vo. Cloth, price 12s.

HAWKINS (Edwards Comerford).
 Spirit and Form. Sermons preached in the parish church of Leatherhead. Crown 8vo. Cloth, price 6s.

HAYES (A. H.).
 New Colorado and the Santa Fé Trail. With map and 60 Illustrations. Crown 8vo. Cloth, price 9s.

HEIDENHAIN (Rudolf), M.D.
 Animal Magnetism. Physiological Observations. Translated from the Fourth German Edition, by L. C. Wooldridge. With a Preface by G. R. Romanes, F.R.S. Crown 8vo. Cloth, price 2s. 6d.

HELLON (H. G.).
 Daphnis. A Pastoral Poem. Small crown 8vo. Cloth.

HELLWALD (Baron F. von).
 The Russians in Central Asia. A Critical Examination, down to the present time, of the Geography and History of Central Asia. Translated by Lieut.-Col. Theodore Wirgman, LL.B. Large post 8vo. With Map. **Cloth,** price 12s.

HELVIG (Major H.).
 The Operations of the Bavarian Army Corps. Translated by Captain G. S. Schwabe. With Five large Maps. In 2 vols. Demy 8vo. Cloth, price 24s.

 Tactical Examples: Vol. I. The Battalion, price 15s. Vol. II. The Regiment and Brigade, price 10s. 6d. Translated from the German by Col. Sir Lumley Graham. With numerous Diagrams. Demy 8vo. Cloth.

HERFORD (Brooke).
 The Story of Religion in England. A Book for Young Folk. Crown 8vo. Cloth, price 5s.

HICKEY (E. H.).
 A Sculptor and other Poems. Small crown 8vo. Cloth, price 5s.

HINTON (James).
 Life and Letters of. Edited by Ellice Hopkins, with an Introduction by Sir W. W. Gull, Bart., and Portrait engraved on Steel by C. H. Jeens. Fourth Edition. Crown 8vo. Cloth, 8s. 6d.

 Chapters **on the Art of** Thinking, and **other** Essays. With an Introduction by Shadworth Hodgson. Edited by C. H. Hinton. Crown 8vo. Cloth, price 8s. 6d.

 The Place of the Physician. To which is added ESSAYS ON THE LAW OF HUMAN LIFE, AND ON THE RELATION BETWEEN ORGANIC AND INORGANIC WORLDS. Second Edition. Crown 8vo. Cloth, price 3s. 6d.

 Physiology for Practical Use. By various Writers. With 50 Illustrations. Third and cheaper edition. Crown 8vo. Cloth, price 5s.

 An Atlas of Diseases of the Membrana Tympani. With Descriptive Text. Post 8vo. Price £6 6s.

 The Questions of Aural Surgery. With Illustrations. 2 vols. Post 8vo. Cloth, price 12s. 6d.

 The Mystery of Pain. New Edition. Fcap. 8vo. Cloth limp, 1s.

HOCKLEY (W. B.).
 Tales of the Zenana; or, A Nuwab's Leisure Hours. By the Author of "Pandurang Hari." With a Preface by Lord Stanley of Alderley. 2 vols. Crown 8vo. Cloth, price 21s.

 Pandurang Hari; or, Memoirs of a Hindoo. A Tale of Mahratta Life sixty years ago. With a Preface by Sir H. Bartle E. Frere, G.C.S.I., &c. New and Cheaper Edition. Crown 8vo. Cloth, price 6s.

HOFFBAUER (Capt.).
 The German Artillery in the Battles near Metz. Based on the official reports of the German Artillery. Translated by Capt. E. O. Hollist. With Map and Plans. Demy 8vo. Cloth, price 21s.

HOLMES (E. G. A.).
 Poems. First and Second Series. Fcap. 8vo. Cloth, price 5s. each.

HOOPER (Mary).
 Little Dinners: How to Serve them with Elegance and Economy. Thirteenth Edition. Crown 8vo. Cloth, price 5s.
 Cookery for Invalids, Persons of Delicate Digestion, and Children. Crown 8vo. Cloth, price 3s. 6d.
 Every-Day Meals. Being Economical and Wholesome Recipes for Breakfast, Luncheon, and Supper. Second Edition. Crown 8vo. Cloth, price 5s.

HOOPER (Mrs. G.).
 The House of Raby. With a Frontispiece. Crown 8vo. Cloth, price 3s. 6d.

HORNER (The Misses).
 Walks in Florence. A New and thoroughly Revised Edition. 2 vols. Crown 8vo. Cloth limp. With Illustrations.
 Vol. I.—Churches, Streets, and Palaces. 10s. 6d. Vol. II.—Public Galleries and Museums. 5s.

Household Readings on Prophecy. By a Layman. Small crown 8vo. Cloth, price 3s. 6d.

HUGHES (Henry).
 The Redemption of the World. Crown 8vo. Cloth, price 3s. 6d.

HULL (Edmund C. P.).
 The European in India. With a MEDICAL GUIDE FOR ANGLO-INDIANS. By R. R. S. Mair, M.D., F.R.C.S.E. Third Edition, Revised and Corrected. Post 8vo. Cloth, price 6s.

HUTCHISON (Lieut.-Col. F. J.), and Capt. G. H. MACGREGOR.
 Military Sketching and Reconnaissance. With Fifteen Plates. Second edition. Small 8vo. Cloth, price 6s.
 The first Volume of Military Handbooks for Regimental Officers. Edited by Lieut.-Col. C. B. BRACKENBURY, R.A., A.A.G.

HUTTON (Arthur), M.A.
 The Anglican Ministry. Its Nature and Value in relation to the Catholic Priesthood. With a Preface by his Eminence Cardinal Newman. Demy 8vo. Cloth, price 14s.

INCHBOLD (J. W.).
 Annus Amoris. Sonnets. Fcap. 8vo. Cloth, price 4s. 6d.

INGELOW (Jean).
 Off the Skelligs. A Novel. With Frontispiece. Second Edition. Crown 8vo. Cloth, price 6s.
 The Little Wonder-horn. A Second Series of "Stories Told to a Child." With Fifteen Illustrations. Small 8vo. Cloth, price 2s. 6d.

International Scientific Series (The). Each book complete in one Volume. Crown 8vo. Cloth, price 5s. each, excepting those marked otherwise.

 I. Forms of Water: A Familiar Exposition of the Origin and Phenomena of Glaciers. By J. Tyndall, LL.D., F.R.S. With 25 Illustrations. Eighth Edition.

 II. Physics and Politics; or, Thoughts on the Application of the Principles of "Natural Selection" and "Inheritance" to Political Society. By Walter Bagehot. Fifth Edition. Crown 8vo. Cloth, price 4s.

 III. Foods. By Edward Smith, M.D., &c. With numerous Illustrations. Seventh Edition.

 IV. Mind and Body: The Theories of their Relation. By Alexander Bain, LL.D. With Four Illustrations. Tenth Edition. Crown 8vo. Cloth, price 4s.

 V. The Study of Sociology. By Herbert Spencer. Tenth Edition.

 VI. On the Conservation of Energy. By Balfour Stewart, LL.D., &c. With 14 Illustrations. Fifth Edition.

 VII. Animal Locomotion; or, Walking, Swimming, and Flying. By J. B. Pettigrew, M.D., &c. With 130 Illustrations. Second Edition.

 VIII. Responsibility in Mental Disease. By Henry Maudsley, M.D. Third Edition.

 IX. The New Chemistry. By Professor J. P. Cooke. With 31 Illustrations. Fifth Edition.

 X. The Science of Law. By Prof. Sheldon Amos. Fourth Edition.

International Scientific Series (The)—*continued*.

XI. Animal Mechanism. A Treatise on Terrestrial and Aerial Locomotion. By Prof. E. J. Marey. With **117** Illustrations. Second Edition.

XII. The Doctrine of Descent and Darwinism. By Prof. Osca Schmidt. With 26 Illustrations. Fourth Edition.

XIII. The History of the Conflict between Religion and Science. By J. W. Draper, M.D., LL.D. Fifteenth Edition.

XIV. Fungi; their Nature, Influences, Uses, &c. By M. C. Cooke, LL.D. Edited by the Rev. M. J. Berkeley, F.L.S. With numerous Illustrations. Second Edition.

XV. The Chemical Effects of Light and Photography. By Dr Hermann Vogel. With 100 Illustrations. Third and Revised Edition.

XVI. The Life and Growth of Language. By Prof. William Dwight Whitney. Third Edition.

XVII. Money and the Mechanism of Exchange. By W. Stanley Jevons, F.R.S. Fourth Edition.

XVIII. The Nature of Light: With a General Account of Physical Optics. By Dr. Eugene Lommel. With 188 Illustrations and a table of Spectra in Chromo-lithography. Third Edition.

XIX. Animal Parasites and Messmates. By M. Van Beneden. With 83 Illustrations. Second Edition.

XX. Fermentation. By Prof. Schützenberger. With 28 Illustrations. Third Edition.

XXI. The Five Senses of Man. By Prof. Bernstein. With 91 Illustrations. Second Edition.

XXII. The Theory of Sound in its Relation to Music. By Prof. Pietro Blaserna. With numerous Illustrations. Second Edition.

XXIII. Studies in Spectrum Analysis. By J. Norman Lockyer. F.R.S. With six photographic Illustrations of Spectra, and numerous engravings on wood. Crown 8vo. Second Edition. 6s. 6d.

International Scientific Series (The)—*continued*.

XXIV. A History of the Growth of the Steam Engine. By Prof. R. H. Thurston. With numerous Illustrations. Second Edition. 6s 6d.

XXV. Education as a Science. By Alexander Bain, LL.D. Third Edition.

XXVI. The Human Species. By Prof. A. de Quatrefages. Third Edition.

XXVII. Modern Chromatics. With Applications to Art and Industry, by Ogden N. Rood. With 130 original Illustrations. Second Edition.

XXVIII. The Crayfish: an Introduction to the Study of Zoology. By Prof. T. H. Huxley. With eighty-two Illustrations. Third edition.

XXIX. **The** Brain as an Organ of Mind. **By** H. Charlton Bastian, M.D. With numerous Illustrations. Second Edition.

XXX. The Atomic Theory. By Prof. Ad. Wurtz. Translated by E. Clemin-Shaw. Second Edition.

XXXI. The Natural Conditions of Existence as they affect Animal Life. By Karl Semper. Second Edition.

XXXII. General Physiology of Muscles and Nerves. By Prof. J. Rosenthal. With Illustrations. Second Edition.

XXXIII. Sight: an Exposition of the Principles of Monocular and Binocular Vision. By Joseph Le Conte, LL.D. With 132 illustrations.

XXXIV. Illusions: A Psychological Study. By James Sully.

XXXV. Volcanoes: What they are and What they Teach. By Prof. J. W. Judd, F.R.S. With 92 Illustrations on Wood.

XXXVI. Suicide. An Essay in Comparative Mythology. By Prof. E. Morselli, with Diagrams.

XXXVII. The Brain and its Functions. By J. Luys. With numerous illustrations.

JENKINS (E.) and RAYMOND (J.).
The Architect's Legal Handbook. Third Edition Revised. Crown 8vo. Cloth, price 6s.

JENKINS (Rev. R. C.), M.A.
The Privilege of Peter and the Claims of the Roman Church confronted with the Scriptures, the Councils, and the Testimony of the Popes themselves. Fcap. 8vo. Cloth, price 3s. 6d.

JENNINGS (Mrs. Vaughan).
Rahel: Her Life and Letters. With a Portrait from the Painting by Daffinger. Square post 8vo. Cloth, price 7s. 6d.

JOEL (L.).
A Consul's Manual and Shipowner's and Shipmaster's Practical Guide in their Transactions Abroad. With Definitions of Nautical, Mercantile, and Legal Terms; a Glossary of Mercantile Terms in English, French, German, Italian, and Spanish. Tables of the Money, Weights, and Measures of the Principal Commercial Nations and their Equivalents in British Standards; and Forms of Consular and Notarial Acts. Demy 8vo. Cloth, price 12s.

JOHNSON (Virginia W.).
The Catskill Fairies. Illustrated by Alfred Fredericks. Cloth, price 5s.

JOHNSTONE (C. F.), M.A.
Historical Abstracts. Being Outlines of the History of some of the less-known States of Europe. Crown 8vo. Cloth, price 7s. 6d.

JONES (Lucy).
Puddings and Sweets. Being Three Hundred and Sixty-Five Receipts approved by Experience. Crown 8vo., price 2s. 6d.

JOYCE (P. W.), LL.D., &c.
Old Celtic Romances. Translated from the Gaelic by. Crown 8vo. Cloth, price 7s. 6d.

KAUFMANN (Rev. M.), B.A.
Utopias; or, Schemes of Social Improvement, from Sir Thomas More to Karl Marx. Crown 8vo. Cloth, price 5s.
Socialism: Its Nature, its Dangers, and its Remedies considered. Crown 8vo. Cloth, price 7s. 6d.

KAY (Joseph), M.A., Q.C.
Free Trade in Land. Edited by his Widow. With Preface by the Right Hon. John Bright, M.P. Sixth Edition. Crown 8vo. Cloth, price 5s.

KEMPIS (Thomas à).
Of the Imitation of Christ. Parchment Library Edition, price 6s.; vellum, price 7s. 6d.
*** A Cabinet Edition is also published at 1s. 6d. and a Miniature Edition at 1s. These may also be had in various extra bindings.

KENT (Carolo).
Corona Catholica ad Petri successoris Pedes Oblata. De Summi Pontificis Leonis XIII. Assumptione Epiggramma. In Quinquaginta Linguis. Fcap. 4to. Cloth, price 15s.

KER (David).
The Boy Slave in Bokhara. A Tale of Central Asia. With Illustrations. Crown 8vo. Cloth, price 3s. 6d.
The Wild Horseman of the Pampas. Illustrated. Crown 8vo. Cloth, price 3s. 6d.

KERNER (Dr. A.), Professor of Botany in the University of Innsbruck.
Flowers and their Unbidden Guests. Translation edited by W. Ogle, M.A., M.D., and a prefatory letter by C. Darwin, F.R.S. With Illustrations. Sq. 8vo. Cloth, price 9s.

KIDD (Joseph), M.D.
The Laws of Therapeutics, or, the Science and Art of Medicine. Second Edition. Crown 8vo. Cloth, price 6s.

KINAHAN (G. Henry), M.R.I.A., &c., of her Majesty's Geological Survey.
Manual of the Geology of Ireland. With 8 Plates, 26 Woodcuts, and a Map of Ireland, geologically coloured. Square 8vo. Cloth, price 15s.

KING (Mrs. Hamilton).
The Disciples. Fourth Edition, with Portrait and Notes. Crown 8vo. Cloth, price 7s. 6d.
Aspromonte, and other Poems. Second Edition. Fcap. 8vo. Cloth, price 4s. 6d.

KINGSFORD (Anna), M.D.
The Perfect Way in Diet. A Treatise advocating a Return to the Natural and Ancient Food of Race. Small crown 8vo. Cloth, price 2s.

KINGSLEY (Charles), M.A.
Letters and Memories of his Life. Edited by his Wife. With 2 Steel engraved Portraits and numerous Illustrations on Wood, and a Facsimile of his Handwriting. Thirteenth Edition. 2 vols. Demy 8vo. Cloth, price 36s.

*** Also the eleventh Cabinet Edition in 2 vols. Crown 8vo. Cloth, price 12s.

All Saints' Day and other Sermons. Second Edition. Crown 8vo. Cloth, 7s. 6d.

True Words for Brave Men: a Book for Soldiers' and Sailors' Libraries. Eighth Edition. Crown 8vo. Cloth, price 2s. 6d.

KNIGHT (Professor W.).
Studies in Philosophy and Literature. Large post 8vo. Cloth, price 7s. 6d.

KNOX (Alexander A.).
The New Playground: or, Wanderings in Algeria. Large crown 8vo. Cloth, price 10s. 6d.

LAMONT (Martha MacDonald).
The Gladiator: A Life under the Roman Empire in the beginning of the Third Century. With four Illustrations by H. M. Paget. Extra fcap. 8vo. Cloth, price 3s. 6d.

LANG (A.).
XXXII Ballades in Blue China. Elzevir. 8vo. Parchment, price 5s.

LAYMANN (Capt.).
The Frontal Attack of Infantry. Translated by Colonel Edward Newdigate. Crown 8vo. Cloth, price 2s. 6d.

LEANDER (Richard).
Fantastic Stories. Translated from the German by Paulina B. Granville. With Eight full-page Illustrations by M. E. Fraser-Tytler. Crown 8vo. Cloth, price 5s.

LEE (Rev. F. G.), D.C.L.
The Other World; or, Glimpses of the Supernatural. 2 vols. A New Edition. Crown 8vo. Cloth, price 15s.

LEE (Holme).
Her Title of Honour. A Book for Girls. New Edition. With a Frontispiece. Crown 8vo. Cloth, price 5s.

LEWIS (Edward Dillon).
A Draft Code of Criminal Law and Procedure. Demy 8vo. Cloth, price 21s.

LEWIS (Mary A.).
A Rat with Three Tales. New and cheaper edition. With Four Illustrations by Catherine F. Frere. Crown 8vo. Cloth, price 3s. 6d.

LINDSAY (W. Lauder), M.D., &c.
Mind in the Lower Animals in Health and Disease. 2 vols. Demy 8vo. Cloth, price 32s.

LOCKER (F.).
London Lyrics. A New and Revised Edition, with Additions and a Portrait of the Author. Crown 8vo. Cloth, elegant, price 6s. Also a Cheap Edition, price 2s. 6d.

LOKI.
The New Werther. Small crown 8vo. Cloth, price 2s. 6d.

LORIMER (Peter), D.D.
John Knox and the Church of England: His Work in her Pulpit, and his Influence upon her Liturgy, Articles, and Parties. Demy 8vo. Cloth, price 12s.

John Wiclif **and his** English Precursors, by Gerhard Victor Lechler. Translated from the German, with additional Notes. New and Cheaper Edition. Demy 8vo. Cloth, price 10s. 6d.

Love Sonnets of Proteus. With frontispiece by the Author. Elzevir 8vo. Cloth, price 5s.

Lowder (Charles): a Biography. By the author of "St. Teresa." Large crown 8vo. With Portrait. Cloth, price 7s. 6d.

LOWNDES (Henry).
Poems and Translations. Crown 8vo. Cloth, price 6s.

LUMSDEN (Lieut.-Col. H. W.).
Beowulf. An Old English Poem. Translated into modern rhymes. Small crown 8vo. Cloth, price 5s.

MAC CLINTOCK (L.).
Sir Spangle and the Dingy Hen. Illustrated. Square crown 8vo., price 2s. 6d.

MACDONALD (G.).
Malcolm. With Portrait of the Author engraved on Steel. Fourth Edition. Crown 8vo. Price 6s.
The Marquis of Lossie. Second Edition. Crown 8vo. Cloth, price 6s.
St. George and St. Michael. Second Edition. Crown 8vo. Cloth, 6s.

MACKENNA (S. J.).
Plucky Fellows. A Book for Boys. With Six Illustrations. Fourth Edition. Crown 8vo. Cloth, price 3s. 6d.
At School with an Old Dragoon. With Six Illustrations. Second Edition. Crown 8vo. Cloth, price 5s.

MACLACHLAN (Mrs.).
Notes and Extracts on Everlasting Punishment and Eternal Life, according to Literal Interpretation. Small crown 8vo. Cloth, price 3s. 6d.

MACLEAN (Charles Donald).
Latin and Greek Verse Translations. Small crown 8vo. Cloth, price 2s.

MACNAUGHT (Rev. John).
Coena Domini: An Essay on the Lord's Supper, its Primitive Institution, Apostolic Uses, and Subsequent History. Demy 8vo. Cloth, price 14s.

MAGNUS (Mrs.).
About the Jews since Bible Times. From the Babylonian exile till the English Exodus. Small crown 8vo. Cloth, price 6s.

MAGNUSSON (Eirikr), M.A., and PALMER (E.H.), M.A.
Johan Ludvig Runeberg's Lyrical Songs, Idylls and Epigrams. Fcap. 8vo. Cloth, price 5s.

MAIR (R. S.), M.D., F.R.C.S.E.
The Medical Guide for Anglo-Indians. Being a Compendium of Advice to Europeans in India, relating to the Preservation and Regulation of Health. With a Supplement on the Management of Children in India. Second Edition. Crown 8vo. Limp cloth, price 3s. 6d.

MALDEN (H. E. and E. E.)
Princes and Princesses. Illustrated. Small crown 8vo. Cloth, price 2s. 6d.

MANNING (His Eminence Cardinal).
The True Story of the Vatican Council. Crown 8vo. Cloth, price 5s.

MARKHAM (Capt. Albert Hastings), R.N.
The Great Frozen Sea. A Personal Narrative of the Voyage of the "Alert" during the Arctic Expedition of 1875-6. With six full-page Illustrations, two Maps, and twenty-seven Woodcuts. Fourth and cheaper edition. Crown 8vo. Cloth, price 6s.
A Polar Reconnaissance: being the Voyage of the "Isbjorn" to Novaya Zemlya in 1879. With 10 Illustrations. Demy 8vo. Cloth, price 16s.

Marriage and Maternity; or, Scripture Wives and Mothers. Small crown 8vo. Cloth, price 4s. 6d.

MARTINEAU (Gertrude).
Outline Lessons on Morals. Small crown 8vo. Cloth, price 3s. 6d.

Master Bobby: a Tale. By the Author of "Christina North." With Illustrations by E. H. Bell. Extra fcap. 8vo. Cloth, price 3s. 6d.

MASTERMAN (J.).
Half-a-dozen Daughters. With a Frontispiece. Crown 8vo. Cloth, price 3s. 6d.

McGRATH (Terence).
Pictures from Ireland. New and cheaper edition. Crown 8vo. Cloth, price 2s.

MEREDITH (George).
The Egoist. A Comedy in Narrative. 3 vols. Crown 8vo. Cloth.
*** Also a Cheaper Edition, with Frontispiece. Crown 8vo. Cloth, price 6s.

The Ordeal of Richard Feverel. A History of Father and Son. In one vol. with Frontispiece. Crown 8vo. Cloth, price 6s.

MEREDITH (Owen) [the Earl of Lytton].
Lucile. With 160 Illustrations. Crown 4to. cloth extra, gilt leaves, price 21s.

MERRITT (Henry).
Art - Criticism and Romance. With Recollections, and Twenty-three Illustrations in eauforte, by Anna Lea Merritt. Two vols. Large post 8vo. Cloth, 25s.

MIDDLETON (The Lady).
Ballads. Square 16mo. Cloth, price 3s. 6d.

MILLER (Edward).
The History and Doctrines of Irvingism; or, the so-called Catholic and Apostolic Church. 2 vols. Large post 8vo. Cloth, price 25s.

The Church in Relation to the State. Crown 8vo. Cloth, price 7s. 6d.

MILNE (James).
Tables of Exchange for the Conversion of Sterling Money into Indian and Ceylon Currency, at Rates from 1s. 8d. to 2s. 3d. per Rupee. Second Edition. Demy 8vo. Cloth, price £2 2s.

MOCKLER (E.).
A Grammar of the Baloochee Language, as it is spoken in Makran (Ancient Gedrosia), in the Persia-Arabic and Roman characters. Fcap. 8vo. Cloth, price 5s.

MOFFAT (Robert Scott).
The Economy of Consumption; an Omitted Chapter in Political Economy, with special reference to the Questions of Commercial Crises and the Policy of Trades Unions; and with Reviews of the Theories of Adam Smith, Ricardo, J. S. Mill, Fawcett, &c. Demy 8vo. Cloth, price 18s.

The Principles of a Time Policy; being an Exposition of a Method of Settling Disputes between Employers and Employed in regard to Time and Wages, by a simple Process of Mercantile Barter, without recourse to Strikes or Locks-out. Demy 8vo. Cloth, price 3s. 6d.

MORELL (J. R.).
Euclid Simplified in Method and Language. Being a Manual of Geometry. Compiled from the most important French Works, approved by the University of Paris and the Minister of Public Instruction. Fcap. 8vo. Cloth, price 2s. 6d.

MORSE (E. S.), Ph.D.
First Book of Zoology. With numerous Illustrations. New and cheaper edition. Crown 8vo. Cloth, price 2s. 6d.

MORSHEAD (E. D. A.).
The House of Atreus. Being the Agamemnon Libation-Bearers and Furies of Æschylus Translated into English Verse. Crown 8vo. Cloth, price 7s.

MUNRO (Major-Gen. Sir Thomas), K.C.B., Governor of Madras.
Selections from His Minutes, and other Official Writings. Edited, with an Introductory Memoir, by Sir Alexander Arbuthnot, K.C.S.I., C.I.E. Two vols. Demy 8vo. Cloth, price 30s.

NAAKE (J. T.).
Slavonic Fairy Tales. From Russian, Servian, Polish, and Bohemian Sources. With Four Illustrations. Crown 8vo. Cloth, price 5s.

NELSON (J. H.).
A Prospectus of the Scientific Study of the Hindû Law. Demy 8vo. Cloth, price 9s.

NEWMAN (J. H.), D.D.
Characteristics from the Writings of. Being Selections from his various Works. Arranged with the Author's personal approval. Third Edition. With Portrait. Crown 8vo. Cloth, price 6s.
₊ A Portrait of the Rev. Dr. J. H. Newman, mounted for framing, can be had, price 2s. 6d.

NICHOLAS (Thomas), Ph.D., F.G.S.
The Pedigree of the English People: an Argument, Historical and Scientific, on the Formation and Growth of the Nation, tracing Race-admixture in Britain from the earliest times, with especial reference to the incorporation of the Celtic Aborigines. Fifth Edition. Demy 8vo. Cloth, price 16s.

NICHOLSON (Edward Byron).
The Christ Child, and other Poems. Crown 8vo. Cloth, price 4s. 6d.

The Rights of an Animal. Crown 8vo. Cloth, price 3s. 6d.

The Gospel according to the Hebrews. Its Fragments translated and annotated, with a critical Analysis of the External and Internal Evidence relating to it. Demy 8vo. Cloth, price 9s. 6d.

A New Commentary on the Gospel according to Matthew. Demy 8vo. Cloth, price 12s.

NICOLS (Arthur), F.G.S., F.R.G.S.
Chapters from the Physical History of the Earth. An Introduction to Geology and Palæontology, with numerous illustrations. Crown 8vo. Cloth, price 5s.

NOAKE (Major R. Compton).
The Bivouac; or, Martial Lyrist, with an Appendix—Advice to the Soldier. Fcap. 8vo. Price 5s. 6d.

NOEL (The Hon. Roden).
A Little Child's Monument. Third Edition. Small crown 8vo. Cloth, price 3s. 6d.

NORMAN PEOPLE (The).
The Norman People, and their Existing Descendants in the British Dominions and the United States of America. Demy 8vo. Cloth, price 21s.

NORRIS (Rev. Alfred).
The Inner and Outer Life Poems. Fcap. 8vo. Cloth, price 6s.

Notes on Cavalry Tactics, Organization, &c. By a Cavalry Officer. With Diagrams. Demy 8vo. Cloth, price 12s.

Nuces: Exercises on the Syntax of the Public School Latin Primer. New Edition in Three Parts. Crown 8vo. Each 1s.
₊ The Three Parts can also be had bound together in cloth, price 3s.

OATES (Frank), F.R.G.S.
Matabele Land and the Victoria Falls: A Naturalist's Wanderings in the Interior of South Africa. Edited by C. G. Oates, B.A., with numerous illustrations and four maps. Demy 8vo. Cloth, price 21s.

O'BRIEN (Charlotte G.).
Light and Shade. 2 vols. Crown 8vo. Cloth, gilt tops, price 12s.

Ode of Life (The).
Third Edition. Fcap. 8vo. Cloth, price 5s.

OF THE IMITATION OF CHRIST. Four Books. Cabinet Edition, price 1s. and 1s. 6d., cloth; Miniature Edition, price 1s.
₊ Also in various bindings.

O'HAGAN (John).
The Song of Roland. Translated into English Verse. Large post 8vo. Parchment antique, price 10s. 6d.

O'MEARA (Kathleen).
Frederic Ozanam, Professor of the Sorbonne; His Life and Works. Second Edition. Crown 8vo. Cloth, price 7s. 6d.

Henri Perreyve and His Counsels to the Sick. Small crown 8vo. Cloth, price 5s.

OTTLEY (Henry Bickersteth).
 The Great Dilemma: Christ His own Witness or His own Accuser. Six Lectures. Crown 8vo. Cloth, price 3s. 6d.

 Our Public Schools. Eton, Harrow, Winchester, Rugby, Westminster, Marlborough, The Charterhouse. Crown 8vo. Cloth, price 6s.

OWEN (F. M.).
 John Keats. A Study. Crown 8vo. Cloth, price 6s.

OWEN (Rev. Robert), B.D.
 Sanctorale Catholicum; or Book of Saints. With Notes, Critical, Exegetical, and Historical. Demy 8vo. Cloth, price 18s.

 An Essay on the Communion of Saints. Including an Examination of the "Cultus Sanctorum." Price 2s.

PALGRAVE (W. Gifford).
 Hermann Agha; An Eastern Narrative. Third and Cheaper Edition. Crown 8vo. Cloth, price 6s.

PANDURANG HARI;
 Or, Memoirs of a Hindoo. With an Introductory Preface by Sir H. Bartle E. Frere, G.C.S.I., C.B. Crown 8vo. Price 6s.

PARCHMENT LIBRARY (The).
Choicely printed on hand-made paper, limp parchment antique, price 6s. each; vellum, price 7s. 6d. each.

 Edgar Allan Poe's Poems. With an Essay on his Poetry by ANDREW LANG and a frontispiece by Linley Sambourne.

 Shakspere's Sonnets. Edited by Edward Dowden. With a Frontispiece, etched by Leopold Lowenstam, after the Death Mask.

 English Odes. Selected by Edmund W. Gosse. With Frontispiece on India paper by Hamo Thornycroft, A.R.A.

 OF THE IMITATION OF CHRIST. Four Books. A revised Translation. With Frontispiece on India paper, from a Design by W. B. Richmond.

PARCHMENT LIBRARY (The)
—*continued.*

 Tennyson's The Princess: a Medley. With a Miniature Frontispiece by H. M. Paget, and a Tailpiece in Outline by Gordon Browne.

 Poems: Selected from Percy Bysshe Shelley. Dedicated to Lady Shelley. With Preface by Richard Garnet, and a Miniature Frontispiece.

 Tennyson's "In Memoriam." With a Miniature Portrait in *eau forte* by Le Rat, after a Photograph by the late Mrs. Cameron.

PARKER (Joseph), D.D.
 The Paraclete: An Essay on the Personality and Ministry of the Holy Ghost, with some reference to current discussions. Second Edition. Demy 8vo. Cloth, price 12s.

PARR (Capt. H. Hallam).
 A Sketch of the Kafir and Zulu Wars: Guadana to Isandhlwana, with Maps. Small crown 8vo. Cloth, price 5s.

 The Dress, Horses, and Equipment of Infantry and Staff Officers. Crown 8vo. Cloth, price 1s.

PARSLOE (Joseph).
 Our Railways: Sketches, Historical and Descriptive. With Practical Information as to Fares, Rates, &c., and a Chapter on Railway Reform. Crown 8vo. Cloth, price 6s.

PATTISON (Mrs. Mark).
 The Renaissance of Art in France. With Nineteen Steel Engravings. 2 vols. Demy 8vo. Cloth, price 32s.

PAUL (C. Kegan).
 Mary Wollstonecraft. Letters to Imlay. With Prefatory Memoir by, and Two Portraits in *eau forte*, by Anna Lea Merritt. Crown 8vo. Cloth, price 6s.

 Goethe's Faust. A New Translation in Rime. Crown 8vo. Cloth, price 6s.

PAUL (C. Kegan)—*continued.*
William Godwin: His Friends and Contemporaries. With Portraits and Facsimiles of the Handwriting of Godwin and his Wife. 2 vols. Square post 8vo. Cloth, price 28s.

The Genius of Christianity Unveiled. Being Essays by William Godwin never before published. Edited, with a Preface, by C. Kegan Paul. Crown 8vo. Cloth, price 7s. 6d.

PAUL (Margaret Agnes).
Gentle and Simple: A Story. 2 vols. **Crown 8vo. Cloth,** gilt tops, price 12s.
*** Also a Cheaper Edition in one vol. **with** Frontispiece. Crown 8vo. **Cloth, price** 6s.

PAYNE (John).
Songs of Life and Death. Crown 8vo. Cloth, price 5s.

PAYNE (Prof. J. F.).
Fröbel and the Kindergarten System. Second Edition.

A Visit to German Schools: Elementary Schools in Germany. Crown 8vo. Cloth, price 4s. 6d.

PELLETAN (E.).
The Desert Pastor, Jean Jarousseau. Translated from the French. By Colonel E. P. De L'Hoste. With a Frontispiece. New Edition. Fcap. 8vo. Cloth, price 3s. 6d.

PENNELL (H. Cholmondeley).
Pegasus Resaddled. By the Author of "Puck on Pegasus," &c. &c. With Ten Full-page Illustrations by George Du Maurier. Second Edition. Fcap. 4to. Cloth elegant, price 12s. 6d.

PENRICE (Maj. J.), B.A.
A Dictionary and Glossary of the Ko-ran. With copious Grammatical References and Explanations of the Text. 4to. Cloth, price 21s.

PESCHEL (Dr. Oscar).
The Races of Man and their Geographical Distribution. Large crown 8vo. Cloth, price 9s.

PETERS (F. H.).
The Nicomachean Ethics of Aristotle. Translated by. Crown 8vo. Cloth, price 6s.

PFEIFFER (Emily).
Under the Aspens. Lyrical and Dramatic. Crown 8vo. With Portrait. Cloth, price 6s.

Quarterman's Grace, and other Poems. Crown 8vo. Cloth, price 5s.

Glan Alarch: His Silence and Song. A Poem. Second Edition. Crown 8vo. price 6s.

Gerard's Monument, and other Poems. Second Edition. Crown 8vo. Cloth, price 6s.

Poems. Second Edition. Crown 8vo. Cloth, price 6s.

Sonnets and Songs. New Edition. 16mo, handsomely printed and bound in cloth, gilt edges, price 5s.

PIKE (Warburton).
The Inferno of Dante Alighieri. Demy 8vo. Cloth, price 5s.

PINCHES (Thomas), M.A.
Samuel Wilberforce: Faith —Service—Recompense. Three Sermons. With a Portrait of Bishop Wilberforce (after a Photograph by Charles Watkins). Crown 8vo. Cloth, price 4s. 6d.

PLAYFAIR (Lieut.-Col.), Her Britannic Majesty's Consul-General in Algiers.
Travels in the Footsteps of Bruce in Algeria and Tunis. Illustrated by facsimiles of Bruce's original Drawings, Photographs, Maps, &c. Royal 4to. Cloth, bevelled boards, gilt leaves, price £3 3s.

POLLOCK (Frederick).
Spinoza. His Life and Philosophy. Demy 8vo. Cloth, price 16s.

POLLOCK (W. H.).
Lectures on French Poets. Delivered at the Royal Institution. Small crown 8vo. Cloth, price 5s.

POOR (Laura E.).
Sanskrit and its kindred Literatures. Studies in Comparative Mythology. Small crown 8vo. Cloth, price 5s.

POUSHKIN (A. S.).
Russian Romance. Translated from the Tales of Belkin, &c. By Mrs. J. Buchan Telfer (née Mouravieff). Crown 8vo. Cloth, price 3s. 6d.

PRESBYTER.
Unfoldings of Christian Hope. An Essay showing that the Doctrine contained in the Damnatory Clauses of the Creed commonly called Athanasian is unscriptural. Small crown 8vo. Cloth, price 4s. 6d.

PRICE (Prof. Bonamy).
Currency and Banking. Crown 8vo. Cloth, price 6s.

Chapters on Practical Political Economy. Being the Substance of Lectures delivered before the University of Oxford. Large post 8vo. Cloth, price 12s.

Proteus and Amadeus. A Correspondence. Edited by Aubrey De Vere. Crown 8vo. Cloth, price 5s.

PUBLIC SCHOOLBOY.
The Volunteer, the Militiaman, and the Regular Soldier. Crown 8vo. Cloth, price 5s.

PULPIT COMMENTARY (The). Edited by the Rev. J. S. Exell and the Rev. Canon H. D. M. Spence.

Genesis. By Rev. T. Whitelaw, M.A.; with Homilies by the Very Rev. J. F. Montgomery, D.D., Rev. Prof. R. A. Redford, M.A., LL.B., Rev. F. Hastings, Rev. W. Roberts, M.A. An Introduction to the Study of the Old Testament by the Rev. Canon Farrar, D.D., F.R.S.; and Introductions to the Pentateuch by the Right Rev. H. Cotterill, D.D., and Rev. T. Whitelaw, M.A. Fifth Edition. Price 15s.

PULPIT COMMENTARY (The) —continued.

Numbers. By the Rev. R. Winterbotham, LL.B. With Homilies by the Rev. Prof. W. Binnie, D.D., Rev. E. S. Prout, M.A., Rev. D. Young, Rev. J. Waite, and an Introduction by the Rev. Thomas Whitelaw, M.A. Third Edition. Price 15s.

Joshua. By the Rev. J. J. Lias, M.A. With Homilies by the Rev. S. R. Aldridge, LL.B., Rev. R. Glover, Rev. E. de Pressensé, D.D., Rev. J. Waite, Rev. F. W. Adeney, and an Introduction by the Rev. A. Plummer, M.A. Third Edition. Price 12s. 6d.

Judges and Ruth. By Right Rev. Lord A. C. Hervey, D.D., and Rev. J. Morrison, D.D. With Homilies by Rev. A. F. Muir, M.A.; Rev. W. F. Adeney, M.A.; Rev. W. M. Statham; and Rev. Prof. J. R. Thomson, M.A. Third Edition. Cloth, price 15s.

1 Samuel. By the Very Rev. R. P. Smith, D.D. With Homilies by the Rev. Donald Fraser, D.D., Rev. Prof. Chapman, and Rev. B. Dale. Fourth Edition. Price 15s.

1 Kings. By the Rev. Joseph Hammond, LL.B. With Homilies by the Rev. E. de Pressensé, D.D., Rev. J. Waite, B.A., Rev. A. Rowland, LL.B., Rev. J. A. Macdonald, and Rev. J. Urquhart.

Ezra, Nehemiah, and Esther. By Rev. Canon G. Rawlinson, M.A.; with Homilies by Rev. Prof. J. R. Thomson, M.A., Rev. Prof. R. A. Redford, LL.B., M.A., Rev. W. S. Lewis, M.A., Rev. J. A. Macdonald, Rev. A. Mackennal, B.A., Rev. W. Clarkson, B.A., Rev. F. Hastings, Rev. W. Dinwiddie, LL.B., Rev. Prof. Rowlands, B.A., Rev. G. Wood, B.A., Rev. Prof. P. C. Barker, LL.B., M.A., and Rev. J. S. Exell. Fifth Edition. Price 12s. 6d.

Punjaub (The) and North Western Frontier of India. By an old Punjaubee. Crown 8vo. Cloth, price 5s.

Rabbi Jeshua. An Eastern Story. Crown 8vo. Cloth, price 3s. 6d.

RADCLIFFE (Frank R. Y.).
  The New Politicus. Small crown 8vo. Cloth, price 2s. 6d.

RAVENSHAW (John Henry), B.C.S.
  Gaur: **Its** Ruins and Inscriptions. Edited with considerable additions and alterations by his Widow. With forty-four photographic illustrations and twenty-five fac-similes of Inscriptions. Super royal 4to. Cloth, 3l. 13s. **6d.**

READ (Carveth).
  On the Theory **of Logic:** An Essay. Crown **8vo.** Cloth, price 6s.
  Realities of the Future Life. Small crown 8vo. Cloth, price 1s. 6d.

REANEY (Mrs. G. S.).
  Blessing and Blessed; a Sketch of Girl Life. New and cheaper Edition. With a frontispiece. Crown 8vo. Cloth, price 3s. 6d.
  Waking and Working; or, from Girlhood to Womanhood. New and cheaper edition. With a Frontispiece. Crown 8vo. Cloth, price 3s. 6d.
  Rose Gurney's Discovery. A Book for Girls, dedicated to their Mothers. Crown 8vo. Cloth, price 3s. 6d.
  English Girls: their **Place** and Power. With a **Preface** by R. W. Dale, M.A., of Birmingham. Third Edition. Fcap. 8vo. Cloth, price 2s. 6d.
  Just Anyone, and other Stories. Three Illustrations. Royal 16mo. Cloth, price 1s. 6d.
  Sunshine Jenny and other Stories. Three Illustrations. Royal 16mo. Cloth, price 1s. 6d.
  Sunbeam Willie, and other Stories. Three Illustrations. Royal 16mo. Cloth, price 1s. 6d.

RENDALL (J. M.).
  Concise Handbook of the Island of Madeira. With plan of Funchal and map of the Island. Fcap. 8vo. Cloth, price 1s. 6d.

REYNOLDS (Rev. J. W.).
  The Supernatural in Nature. A Verification by Free Use of Science. Second Edition, revised and enlarged. Demy 8vo. Cloth, price 14s.
  Mystery of Miracles, The. By the Author of "The Supernatural in Nature." New and Enlarged Edition. Crown **8vo.** Cloth, price 6s.

RHOADES (James).
  The Georgics of Virgil. Translated into English Verse. Small crown 8vo. Cloth, price 5s.

RIBOT (Prof. Th.).
  English Psychology. Second Edition. A Revised and Corrected Translation from the latest French Edition. Large post 8vo. Cloth, price 9s.
  Heredity: A Psychological Study on its Phenomena, its Laws, its Causes, and its Consequences. Large crown 8vo. Cloth, price 9s.

RINK (Chevalier Dr. Henry).
  Greenland: Its People and its Products. By the Chevalier Dr. HENRY RINK, President of the Greenland Board of Trade. With sixteen Illustrations, drawn by the Eskimo, and a Map. Edited by Dr. ROBERT BROWN. Crown 8vo. Price 10s. 6d.

ROBERTSON (The Late Rev. F. W.), M.A., of Brighton.
  The Human Race, and other Sermons preached at Cheltenham, Oxford, and Brighton. Second Edition. Large post 8vo. Cloth, price 7s. 6d.
  Notes on Genesis. New and cheaper Edition. Crown 8vo., price 3s. 6d.
  Sermons. Four Series. Small crown 8vo. Cloth, price 3s. 6d. each.
  Expository Lectures on St. Paul's Epistles to the Corinthians. A New Edition. Small crown 8vo. Cloth, price 5s.
  Lectures and Addresses, with other literary remains. A New Edition. Crown 8vo. Cloth, price 5s.

ROBERTSON (The Late Rev. F. W.), M.A., of Brighton—continued.
An Analysis of Mr. Tennyson's "In Memoriam." (Dedicated by Permission to the Poet-Laureate.) Fcap. 8vo. Cloth, price 2s.
The Education of the Human Race. Translated from the German of Gotthold Ephraim Lessing. Fcap. 8vo. Cloth, price 2s. 6d.
Life and Letters. Edited by the Rev. Stopford Brooke, M.A., Chaplain in Ordinary to the Queen.
I. 2 vols., uniform with the Sermons. With Steel Portrait. Crown 8vo. Cloth, price 7s. 6d.
II. Library Edition, in Demy 8vo., with Portrait. Cloth, price 12s.
III. A Popular Edition, in one vol. Crown 8vo. Cloth, price 6s.

The above Works can also be had half-bound in morocco.

*** A Portrait of the late Rev. F. W. Robertson, mounted for framing, can be had, price 2s. 6d.

ROBINSON (A. Mary F.).
A Handful of Honeysuckle. Fcap. 8vo. Cloth, price 3s. 6d.
The Crowned Hippolytus. Translated from Euripides. With New Poems. Small crown 8vo. Cloth, price 5s.

RODWELL (G. F.), F.R.A.S., F.C.S.
Etna: a History of the Mountain and its Eruptions. With Maps and Illustrations. Square 8vo. Cloth, price 9s.

ROLLESTON (T. W. H.), B.A.
The Encheiridion of Epictetus. Translated from the Greek, with a Preface and Notes. Small crown 8vo. Cloth, price 3s. 6d.

ROSS (Mrs. E.), ("Nelsie Brook").
Daddy's Pet. A Sketch from Humble Life. With Six Illustrations. Royal 16mo. Cloth, price 1s.

SADLER (S. W.), R.N.
The African Cruiser. A Midshipman's Adventures on the West Coast. With Three Illustrations. Second Edition. Crown 8vo. Cloth, price 3s. 6d.

SALTS (Rev. Alfred), LL.D.
Godparents at Confirmation. With a Preface by the Bishop of Manchester. Small crown 8vo. Cloth, limp, price 2s.

SALVATOR (Archduke Ludwig).
Levkosia, the Capital of Cyprus. Crown 8vo. Cloth, price 10s. 6d.

SAMUEL (Sydney Montagu).
Jewish Life in the East. Small crown 8vo. Cloth, price 3s. 6d.

SAUNDERS (John).
Israel Mort, Overman: A Story of the Mine. Cr. 8vo. Price 6s.
Hirell. With Frontispiece. Crown 8vo. Cloth, price 3s. 6d.
Abel Drake's Wife. With Frontispiece. Crown 8vo. Cloth, price 3s. 6d.

SAYCE (Rev. Archibald Henry).
Introduction to the Science of Language. Two vols., large post 8vo. Cloth, price 25s.

SCHELL (Maj. von).
The Operations of the First Army under Gen. von Goeben. Translated by Col. C. H. von Wright. Four Maps. Demy 8vo. Cloth, price 9s.
The Operations of the First Army under Gen. von Steinmetz. Translated by Captain E. O. Hollist. Demy 8vo. Cloth, price 10s. 6d.

SCHELLENDORF (Maj.-Gen. B. von).
The Duties of the General Staff. Translated from the German by Lieutenant Hare. Vol. I. Demy 8vo. Cloth, 10s. 6d.

SCHERFF (Maj. W. von).
Studies in the New Infantry Tactics. Parts I. and II. Translated from the German by Colonel Lumley Graham. Demy 8vo. Cloth, price 7s. 6d.

Scientific Layman. The New Truth and the Old Faith: are they Incompatible? Demy 8vo. Cloth, price 10s. 6d.

SCOONES (W. Baptiste).
Four Centuries of English Letters. A Selection of 350 Letters by 150 Writers from the period of the Paston Letters to the Present Time. Edited and arranged by. Second Edition. Large crown 8vo. Cloth, price 9s.

SCOTT (Leader).
A Nook in the Apennines: A Summer beneath the Chestnuts. With Frontispiece, and 27 Illustrations in the Text, chiefly from Original Sketches. Crown 8vo. Cloth, price 7s. 6d. Also a Cheap Edition, price 2s. 6d.

SCOTT (Robert H.).
Weather Charts and Storm Warnings. Illustrated. Second Edition. Crown 8vo. Cloth, price 3s. 6d.

Seeking his Fortune, and other Stories. With Four Illustrations. New and cheaper Edition. Crown 8vo. Cloth, price 2s. 6d.

SENIOR (N. W.).
Alexis De Tocqueville. Correspondence and Conversations with Nassau W. Senior, from 1833 to 1859. Edited by M. C. M. Simpson. 2 vols. Large post 8vo. Cloth, price 21s.

Seven Autumn Leaves from Fairyland. Illustrated with Nine Etchings. Square crown 8vo. Cloth, price 3s. 6d.

SHADWELL (Maj.-Gen.), C.B.
Mountain Warfare. Illustrated by the Campaign of 1799 in Switzerland. Being a Translation of the Swiss Narrative compiled from the Works of the Archduke Charles, Jomini, and others. Also of Notes by General H. Dufour on the Campaign of the Valtelline in 1635. With Appendix, Maps, and Introductory Remarks. Demy 8vo. Cloth, price 16s.

SHAKSPEARE (Charles).
Saint Paul at Athens: Spiritual Christianity in Relation to some Aspects of Modern Thought. Nine Sermons preached at St. Stephen's Church, Westbourne Park. With Preface by the Rev. Canon Farrar. Crown 8vo. Cloth, price 5s.

SHAW (Major Wilkinson).
The Elements of Modern Tactics. Practically applied to English Formations. With Twenty-five Plates and Maps. Second and cheaper Edition. Small crown 8vo. Cloth, price 9s.
*** The Second Volume of "Military Handbooks for Officers and Non-commissioned Officers." Edited by Lieut.-Col. C. B. Brackenbury, R.A., A.A.G.

SHAW (Flora L.).
Castle Blair: a Story of Youthful Lives. 2 vols. Crown 8vo. Cloth, gilt tops, price 12s. Also, an dition in one vol. Crown 8vo. 6s.

SHELLEY (Lady).
Shelley Memorials from Authentic Sources. With (now first printed) an Essay on Christianity by Percy Bysshe Shelley. With Portrait. Third Edition. Crown 8vo. Cloth, price 5s.

SHERMAN (Gen. W. T.).
Memoirs of General W. T. Sherman, Commander of the Federal Forces in the American Civil War. By Himself. 2 vols. With Map. Demy 8vo. Cloth, price 24s. *Copyright English Edition.*

SHILLITO (Rev. Joseph).
Womanhood: its Duties, Temptations, and Privileges. A Book for Young Women. Second Edition. Crown 8vo. Price 3s. 6d.

SHIPLEY (Rev. Orby), M.A.
Principles of the Faith in Relation to Sin. Topics for Thought in Times of Retreat. Eleven Addresses. With an Introduction on the neglect of Dogmatic Theology in the Church of England, and a Postscript on his leaving the Church of England. Demy 8vo. Cloth, price 12s.

Church Tracts, or Studies in Modern Problems. By various Writers. 2 vols. Crown 8vo. Cloth, price 5s. each.

Sister Augustine, Superior of the Sisters of Charity at the St. Johannis Hospital at Bonn. Authorized Translation by Hans Tharau from the German Memorials of Amalie von Lasaulx. Second edition. Large crown 8vo. Cloth, price 7s. 6d.

Six Ballads about King Arthur. Crown 8vo. Cloth extra, gilt edges, price 3s. 6d.

SKINNER (James).
Cœlestia: the Manual of St. Augustine. The Latin Text side by side with an English Interpretation, in 36 Odes, with Notes, and a plea for the Study of Mystic Theology. Large crown 8vo. Cloth, price 6s.

SMITH (Edward), M.D., LL.B., F.R.S.
Health and Disease, as Influenced by the Daily, Seasonal, and other Cyclical Changes in the Human System. A New Edition. Post 8vo. Cloth, price 7s. 6d.

Practical Dietary for Families, Schools, and the Labouring Classes. A New Edition. Post 8vo. Cloth, price 3s. 6d.

Tubercular Consumption in its Early and Remediable Stages. Second Edition. Crown 8vo. Cloth, price 6s.

Songs of Two Worlds. By the Author of "The Epic of Hades." Sixth Edition. Complete in one Volume, with Portrait. Fcap. 8vo. Cloth, price 7s. 6d.

Songs for Music.
By Four Friends. Square crown 8vo. Cloth, price 5s.
Containing songs by Reginald A. Gatty, Stephen H. Gatty, Greville J. Chester, and Juliana Ewing.

SPEDDING (James).
Evenings with a Reviewer; or, Bacon and Macaulay. With a Prefatory Notice by G. S. Venables, Q.C. 3 vols. Demy 8vo. Cloth, price 18s.

Reviews and Discussions, Literary, Political, and Historical, not relating to Bacon. Demy 8vo. Cloth, price 12s. 6d.

STAPFER (Paul).
Shakspeare and Classical Antiquity: Greek and Latin Anti-

STAPFER (Paul)—continued.
quity as presented in Shakspeare's Plays. Translated by Emily J. Carey. Large post 8vo. Cloth, price 12s.

St. Bernard on the Love of God. Translated by Marianne Caroline and Coventry Patmore. Cloth extra, gilt top, price 4s. 6d.

STEDMAN (Edmund Clarence).
Lyrics and Idylls. With other Poems. Crown 8vo. Cloth, price 7s. 6d.

STEPHENS (Archibald John), LL.D.
The Folkestone Ritual Case. The Substance of the Argument delivered before the Judicial Committee of the Privy Council. On behalf of the Respondents. Demy 8vo. Cloth, price 6s.

STEVENSON (Robert Louis).
Virginibus, Puerisque, and other Papers. Crown 8vo. Cloth, price 6s.

STEVENSON (Rev. W. F.).
Hymns for the Church and Home. Selected and Edited by the Rev. W. Fleming Stevenson.

The most complete Hymn Book published.

The Hymn Book consists of Three Parts:—I. For Public Worship.—II. For Family and Private Worship.—III. For Children.

*** Published in various forms and prices, the latter ranging from 8d. to 6s. Lists and full particulars will be furnished on application to the Publishers.

STOCKTON (Frank R.).
A Jolly Fellowship. With 20 Illustrations. Crown 8vo. Cloth, price 5s.

STORR (Francis), and TURNER Hawes).
Canterbury Chimes; or, Chaucer Tales retold to Children. With Illustrations from the Ellesmere MS. Extra Fcap. 8vo. Cloth, price 3s. 6d.

Strecker-Wishcenus's Organic Chemistry. Translated and edited with extensive additions by W. R. HODGKINSON, Ph. D., and A. J. GREENWAY, F.I.C. Demy 8vo. Cloth, price 21s.

STRETTON (Hesba).
David Lloyd's Last Will. With Four Illustrations. Royal 16mo., price 2s. 6d.

The Wonderful Life. Thirteenth Thousand. Fcap. 8vo. Cloth, price 2s. 6d.

Through a Needle's Eye: a Story. Crown 8vo. Cloth, price 6s.

STUBBS (Lieut.-Colonel F. W.) The Regiment of Bengal Artillery. The History of its Organization, Equipment, and War Services. Compiled from Published Works, Official Records, and various Private Sources. With numerous Maps and Illustrations. 2 vols. Demy 8vo. Cloth, price 32s.

STUMM (Lieut. Hugo), German Military Attaché to the Khivan Expedition.
Russia's advance Eastward. Based on the Official Reports of. Translated by Capt. C. E. H. VINCENT. With Map. Crown 8vo. Cloth, price 6s.

SULLY (James), M.A.
Sensation and Intuition. Demy 8vo. Second Edition. Cloth, price 10s. 6d.
Pessimism: a History and a Criticism. Demy 8vo. Price 14s.

Sunnyland Stories. By the Author of "Aunt Mary's Bran Pie." Illustrated. Small 8vo. Cloth, price 3s. 6d

Sweet Silvery Sayings of Shakespeare. Crown 8vo. Cloth gilt, price 7s. 6d.

SYME (David).
Outlines of an Industrial Science. Second Edition. Crown 8vo. Cloth, price 6s.

SYME (David)—*continued.*
Representative Government in England. Its Faults and Failures. Large crown 8vo. Cloth, price 6s.

Tales from Ariosto. Retold for Children, by a Lady. With three illustrations. Crown 8vo. Cloth, price 4s. 6d.

TAYLOR (Algernon).
Guienne. Notes of an Autumn Tour. Crown 8vo. Cloth, price 4s. 6d.

TAYLOR (Sir H.).
Works Complete. Author's Edition, in 5 vols. Crown 8vo. Cloth, price 6s. each.
Vols. I. to III. containing the Poetical Works, Vols. IV. and V. the Prose Works.

TAYLOR (Col. Meadows), C.S.I., M.R.I.A.
A Noble Queen: a Romance of Indian History. New Edition. With Frontispiece. Crown 8vo. Cloth. Price 6s.
Seeta. New Edition with frontispiece. Crown 8vo. Cloth, price 6s.
Tippoo Sultaun: a Tale of the Mysore War. New Edition with Frontispiece. Crown 8vo. Cloth, price 6s.
Ralph Darnell. New Edition. With Frontispiece. Crown 8vo. Cloth, price 6s.
The Confessions of a Thug. New Edition. With Frontispiece. Crown 8vo. Cloth, price 6s.
Tara: a Mahratta Tale. New Edition. With Frontispiece. Crown 8vo. Cloth, price 6s.

TENNYSON (Alfred).
The Imperial Library Edition. Complete in 7 vols. Demy 8vo. Cloth, price £3 13s. 6d.; in Roxburgh binding, £4 7s. 6d.

Author's Edition. Complete in 7 Volumes. With Frontispieces. Crown 8vo. Cloth, price 43s. 6d.; Roxburgh half morocco, price 54s.

TENNYSON (Alfred)—*continued.*

Cabinet Edition, in 13 vols. with Frontispieces. Fcap. 8vo. Cloth, price 2s. 6d. each, or complete in cloth box, price 35s.

*** Each volume in the above editions may be had separately.

The Royal Edition. With 26 Illustrations and Portrait. Cloth extra, bevelled boards, gilt leaves. Price 21s.

The Guinea Edition. In 14 vols., neatly bound and enclosed in box. Cloth, price 21s. French morocco or parchment, price 31s. 6d.

The Shilling Edition of the Poetical and Dramatic Works, in 12 vols., pocket size. Price 1s. each.

The Crown Edition [the 118th thousand], strongly bound in cloth, price 6s. Cloth, extra gilt leaves, price 7s. 6d. Roxburgh, half morocco, price 8s. 6d.

*** Can also be had in a variety of other bindings.

Original Editions:

Ballads and other Poems. Fcap. 8vo. Cloth, price 5s.

The Lover's Tale. (Now for the first time published.) Fcap. 8vo. Cloth, 3s. 6d.

Poems. Small 8vo. Cloth, price 6s.

Maud, and other Poems. Small 8vo. Cloth, price 3s. 6d.

The Princess. Small 8vo. Cloth, price 3s. 6d.

Idylls of the King. Small 8vo. Cloth, price 5s.

Idylls of the King. Complete. Small 8vo. Cloth, price 6s.

The Holy Grail, and other Poems. Small 8vo. Cloth, price 4s. 6d.

Gareth and Lynette. Small 8vo. Cloth, price 3s.

Enoch Arden, &c. Small 8vo. Cloth, price 3s. 6d.

TENNYSON (Alfred)—*continued.*

In Memoriam. Small 8vo. Cloth, price 4s.

Queen Mary. A Drama. New Edition. Crown 8vo. Cloth, price 6s.

Harold. A Drama. Crown 8vo. Cloth, price 6s.

Selections from Tennyson's Works. Super royal 16mo. Cloth, price 3s. 6d. Cloth gilt extra, price 4s.

Songs from Tennyson's Works. Super royal 16mo. Cloth extra, price 3s. 6d.

Also a cheap edition. 16mo. Cloth, price 2s. 6d.

Idylls of the King, and other Poems. Illustrated by Julia Margaret Cameron. 2 vols. Folio. Half-bound morocco, cloth sides, price £6 6s. each.

Tennyson for the Young and for Recitation. Specially arranged. Fcap. 8vo. Price 1s. 6d.

Tennyson Birthday Book. Edited by Emily Shakespear. 32mo. Cloth limp, 2s.; cloth extra, 3s.

*** A superior edition, printed in red and black, on antique paper, specially prepared. Small crown 8vo. Cloth extra, gilt leaves, price 5s.; and in various calf and morocco bindings.

Songs Set to Music, by various Composers. Edited by W. G. Cusins. Dedicated by express permission to Her Majesty the Queen. Royal 4to. Cloth extra, gilt leaves, price 21s., or in half-morocco, price 25s.

An Index to "In Memoriam." Price 2s.

THOMAS (Moy).

A Fight for Life. With Frontispiece. Crown 8vo. Cloth, price 3s. 6d.

THOMPSON (Alice C.).

Preludes. A Volume of Poems. Illustrated by Elizabeth Thompson (Painter of "The Roll Call"). 8vo. Cloth, price 7s. 6d.

THOMSON (J. Turnbull).
Social Problems; or, an Inquiry into the Law of Influences. With Diagrams. Demy 8vo. Cloth, price 10s. 6d.

THRING (Rev. Godfrey), B.A.
Hymns and Sacred Lyrics. Fcap. 8vo. Cloth, price 3s. 6d.

TODHUNTER (Dr. J.)
Forest Songs. Small crown 8vo. Cloth, 3s. 6d.
The True Tragedy of Rienzi. A Drama.
A Study of Shelley. Crown 8vo. Cloth, price 7s.
Alcestis: A Dramatic Poem. Extra fcap. 8vo. Cloth, price 5s.
Laurella; and other Poems. Crown 8vo. Cloth, price 6s. 6d.
Translations from Dante, Petrarch, Michael Angelo, and Vittoria Colonna. Fcap. 8vo. Cloth, price 7s. 6d.

TURNER (Rev. C. Tennyson).
Sonnets, Lyrics, and Translations. Crown 8vo. Cloth, price 4s. 6d.
Collected Sonnets, Old and New. With Prefatory Poem by Alfred Tennyson; also some Marginal Notes by S. T. Coleridge, and a Critical Essay by James Spedding. Fcap. 8vo. Cloth, price 7s. 6d.

TWINING (Louisa).
Recollections of Workhouse Visiting and Management during twenty-five years. Small crown 8vo. Cloth, price 3s. 6d.

UPTON (Major R. D.).
Gleanings from the Desert of Arabia. Large post 8vo. Cloth, price 10s. 6d.

VAUGHAN (H. Halford).
New Readings and Renderings of Shakespeare's Tragedies. 2 vols. Demy 8vo. Cloth, price 25s.

VIATOR (Vacuus).
Flying South. Recollections of France and its Littoral. Small crown 8vo. Cloth, price 3s. 6d.

VILLARI (Prof.).
Niccolo Machiavelli and His Times. Translated by Linda Villari. 2 vols. Large post 8vo. Cloth, price 24s.

VINCENT (Capt. C. E. H.).
Elementary Military Geography, Reconnoitring, and Sketching. Square crown 8vo. Cloth, price 2s. 6d.

VYNER (Lady Mary).
Every day a Portion. Adapted from the Bible and the Prayer Book. Square crown 8vo. Cloth extra, price 5s.

WALDSTEIN (Charles), Ph. D.
The Balance of Emotion and Intellect: An Essay Introductory to the Study of Philosophy. Crown 8vo. Cloth, price 6s.

WALLER (Rev. C. B.)
The Apocalypse, Reviewed under the Light of the Doctrine of the Unfolding Ages and the Restitution of all Things. Demy 8vo. Cloth, price 12s.

WALSHE (Walter Hayle), M.D.
Dramatic Singing Physiologically Estimated. Crown 8vo. Cloth, price 3s. 6d.

WALTERS (Sophia Lydia).
The Brook: A Poem. Small crown 8vo. Cloth, price 3s. 6d.
A Dreamer's Sketch Book. With Twenty-one Illustrations. Fcap. 4to. Cloth, price 12s. 6d.

WATERFIELD, W.
Hymns for Holy Days and Seasons. 32mo. Cloth, price 1s. 6d.

WATSON (Sir Thomas), Bart., M.D.
The Abolition of Zymotic Diseases, and of other similar enemies of Mankind. Small crown 8vo. Cloth, price 3s. 6d.

WAY (A.), M.A.
The Odes of Horace Literally Translated in Metre. Fcap. 8vo. Cloth, price 2s.

WEBSTER (Augusta).
Disguises. A Drama. Small crown 8vo. Cloth, price 5s.

WEDMORE (Frederick).
The Masters of Genre Painting. With sixteen illustrations. Large crown 8vo. Cloth, price 7s. 6d.

WHEWELL (William), D.D.
His Life and Selections from his Correspondence. By Mrs. Stair Douglas. With Portrait. Demy 8vo. Cloth, price 21s.

WHITAKER (Florence).
Christy's Inheritance. A London Story. Illustrated. Royal 16mo. Cloth, price 1s. 6d.

WHITE (A. D.), LL.D.
Warfare of Science. With Prefatory Note by Professor Tyndall. Second Edition. Crown 8vo. Cloth, price 3s. 6d.

WHITNEY (Prof. W. D.)
Essentials of English Grammar for the Use of Schools. Crown 8vo. Cloth, price 3s. 6d.

WICKSTEED (P. H.).
Dante: Six Sermons. Crown 8vo. Cloth, price 5s.

WILKINS (William).
Songs of Study. Crown 8vo. Cloth, price 6s.

WILLIAMS (Rowland), D.D.
Stray Thoughts from his Note-Books. Edited by his Widow. Crown 8vo. Cloth, price 3s. 6d.

Psalms, Litanies, Counsels and Collects for Devout Persons. Edited by his Widow. Crown 8vo. Cloth, price 3s. 6d.

WILLIS (R.), M.D.
Servetus and Calvin: a Study of an Important Epoch in the Early History of the Reformation. 8vo. Cloth, price 16s.

William Harvey. A History of the Discovery of the Circulation of the Blood. With a Portrait of Harvey, after Faithorne. Demy 8vo. Cloth, price 14s.

WILSON (Sir Erasmus).
Egypt of the Past. With Illustrations in the Text. Crown 8vo. Cloth, price 12s.

WILSON (H. Schütz).
The Tower and Scaffold. Large fcap. 8vo. Price 1s.

Within Sound of the Sea. By the Author of "Blue Roses," "Vera," &c. Fourth Edition in one vol. with frontispiece. Price 6s.

WOLLSTONECRAFT (Mary).
Letters to Imlay. With a Preparatory Memoir by C. Kegan Paul, and two Portraits in *eau forte* by Anna Lea Merritt. Crown 8vo. Cloth, price 6s.

WOLTMANN (Dr. Alfred), and WOERMANN (Dr. Karl).
History of Painting in Antiquity and the Middle Ages. Edited by Sidney Colvin. With numerous illustrations. Medium 8vo. Cloth, price 28s.; cloth, bevelled boards, gilt leaves, price 30s.

WOOD (Major-General J. Creighton).
Doubling the Consonant. Small crown 8vo. Cloth, price 1s. 6d.

Word was made Flesh. Short Family Readings on the Epistles for each Sunday of the Christian Year. Demy 8vo. Cloth, price 10s. 6d.

Wren (Sir Christopher); his Family and his Times. With Original Letters, and a Discourse on Architecture hitherto unpublished. By Lucy Phillimore. Demy 8vo. With Portrait, price 14s.

WRIGHT (Rev. David), M.A.
Waiting for the Light, and other Sermons. Crown 8vo. Cloth, price 6s.

YOUMANS (Eliza A.).
An Essay on the Culture of the Observing Powers of Children. Crown 8vo. Cloth, price 2s. 6d.

First Book of Botany. With 300 Engravings. Crown 8vo. Cloth, price 2s. 6d.

YOUMANS (Edward L.), M.D.
A Class Book of Chemistry. With 200 Illustrations. Crown 8vo. Cloth, price 5s.

LONDON:—C. KEGAN PAUL & CO., 1, PATERNOSTER SQUARE.

www.ingramcontent.com/pod-product-compliance
Lightning Source LLC
Chambersburg PA
CBHW020104170426
43199CB00009B/384